A Living Lent

*a contemplative daily companion for
Lent and Holy Week*

Peter Traben Haas

A publication of  *ContemplativeChristians.com*

"Then Jesus was led up by the Spirit into the wilderness..."

   – Matthew 4.1

"You desire truth in the inward being..."

   – Psalm 51.6

A Living Lent

*a contemplative daily companion for
Lent and Holy Week*

Published by *ContemplativeChristians.com*

A Living Lent: A contemplative daily companion for Lent and Holy Week
Revised Edition © 2017 Peter Traben Haas
All rights reserved. First Published 2014.

Library of Congress Cataloging-in-Publication Data

Haas, Peter Traben (1972 –   )
A Living Lent: a daily companion for lent and holy week
/ Peter Traben Haas
p.cm.
  ISBN-13: 13: 978-1523301843 (alk. Paper)
  1. Spiritual life – Christianity. 2. Devotional. I. Title.

    BV 4501.3.H33 2014

          20100

    Printed in the United States of America

╬ *Dedicated to:*

Tim and Barbara Cook – teachers, mentors, friends

╬ *Contents*

✠ *Preface*

The season of Lent is an opportunity to experience the fullness of being human and request the grace of becoming Christ, a participant in the divine nature (2 Peter 1.4).

Shadowing Jesus' 40 days of temptation in the wilderness (Matthew 4. 1-11), the Christian tradition counts 40 days of Lent, beginning the day after Ash Wednesday and concluding with Good Friday. Since Sundays are always "little feast days" celebrating the Resurrection, they are not counted in the 40 days of Lent.

However, in this *living lent* daily devotional, I have provided a daily reflection for *all* of the calendar days beginning with Ash Wednesday and concluding with Easter Sunday. The Lenten Tradition invites us to increase and deepen a practice of prayer, fasting and almsgiving, which is the three-fold human spectrum of being: spiritual, physical and social.

We deepen our practice of prayer through setting time aside that we normally would give to something else. We listen and consent to God's presence in the silence. We deepen our practice of fasting by giving up money and time that we normally would give to food, shopping, media or whatever it is we are fasting from, and use that time, energy and attention to nurture our relationship with God. We deepen our practice of caring for others by taking extra time out of our schedule to visit the sick, poor, orphans, widows and those imprisoned. We do *not* do this to be "good little boys and girls," or to do God a favor.

We do this to re-discover and remember our human nature, realizing just how much of our energy, time and resources are spent on taking care of ourselves.

Redistributing our time, energy and resources in this Lenten way, perhaps we may begin to open more fully to a space for grace that enters into our lives in ways we can't imagine. It may even bring deeper healing, transformation and such spiritual fruits as expanded love and wisdom. The space for grace in the silence opens us to the mind of Christ where anything is possible.

As you read these daily reflections during your Lenten journey, my prayer is that the Spirit of God will lead you deeper into the wilderness of your human nature to rediscover the power of the Word of God sustaining you in the barren places of sheer surrender to and within the divine mystery rather than your own personal power, control, plans and capacities, transforming your human nature into Christ.

Every blessing in God's love.

╬ *a living lent*

"On account of God's immense love, God was made [in Christ] what we are to make us what he is."

– St. Irenaeus
Against Heresies

"God was made human so that we might become God [in Christ]."
– St. Athanasius
On the Incarnation

"God assumed a human being in order to make human beings divine."
– St. Augustine
Sermons

A Living Lent // Ash Wednesday

╫

Ashen Prayers

We start Lent with an ashen smudge. It is a simple gesture of connecting us with the confession that we will return to the dust of the earth. We are, like all created living beings, mortal. The season of Lent is a time to pause and follow Jesus' journey of releasing, not grasping. It is a season to release our over-consumption, over-busyness and over-commitments and remember that in God's love everything is perfect. No striving is needed. No grasping is called for. We are invited to a simple alternative to the program for grasping for happiness in all its forms – survival, security, power, control, wealth, affection and fame. We are invited to "*be still before the Lord and wait patiently*" (Psalm 37.7).

In Lent, we discover this is not easy for us. We discover in the silence and solitude that there is a lot going on in our bodies and minds – many voices, many thoughts, many sensations, many desires and, yes, many temptations. And we may feel uncomfortable in the process of this self-discovery.

Because of our human condition, we may resist God's invitation to the spiritual journey and give in to what is easy, comfortable, and our normal patterns for meeting our personal needs through shopping, watching TV, being entertained, sex, eating, going here and there, or even serving. It is not that these activities are bad in and of themselves. The question is: Where are we looking for our happiness? What are we giving our attention to?

As we read the Gospels during Lent, we will discover that Jesus understands and experienced our human condition. Jesus also gave us a model by which to follow as we confront the human condition and our overwhelming needs, demands and addictions for security, power and fame. That model was to know Truth in the face of temptation, or to put it another way, "*to have the mind of Christ*" (Philippians 2.5-11) by "*letting the word of God dwell richly in you*" (Colossians 3.16).

What ends up happening in our human development as we emerge into the world as vulnerable infants and grow into our childhood, adolescence and adulthood is that we begin to develop programs for providing for our own happiness (blessings) apart from God, along the three primary lines of normal human needs:

Survival and security

Affection and esteem

Power and control

Now notice the similar pattern to Jesus' temptations:

Turn stone into bread = *the temptation to take care of himself apart from God.*

Jump off the tallest building in Jerusalem = *the temptation to show off and gain fame.*

Bow down and receive power of the kingdoms = *the temptation to take power.*

Another word for happiness is "blessing." Remember also the wisdom of the Westminster Confession: The chief end of humankind is to love God and enjoy God forever. This idea of enjoyment is closely connected with our pursuit of happiness; however we often overlook the giver and focus on the gifts. Perhaps this calls to mind a much-loved Psalm: *"Happy are those...whose delight is in the law of the Lord, and on this Word they meditate day and night. They are like flourishing trees planted by streams of water, fruitful in every season. In all they do, they prosper."* Psalm 1.1-3 (my translation). As we begin our Lenten journey together, we do so recognizing our need for help with our human condition. While it is the same for all of us, it also plays out in very unique and particular ways. Through this Lenten devotional we are asking God to give us clear self-insight and grace to follow Jesus so to discover Christ.

A Living Lent [Day 1] *Thursday*

╬

If Anyone Wishes

It is Thursday of the first week of Lent. Our inward journey into the Lenten wilderness is just beginning.

The lectionary reading for today sets the tone and theme for our entire Lenten experience. The passage is an inner compass. Jesus' invitation is our True North – a guide that we often question and persistently resist. His words offer a fierce topography that most would rather avoid. And yet, it calls to us.

So, we begin our journey pausing in the stillness and silence of this late winter day, aware that something is coming to life through our surrender. Awake to the peculiar opportunity that is the Lenten inner cross of transformation. A season of further self-discovery through renunciation that may lead us to a deepened life. Listen again, and feel the gravity of the Lenten invitation. Consider the cost. Examine your wish. Plumb your desire:

"Then Jesus said to all, 'If anyone wishes to come after me, he must deny himself and take up his cross daily and follow me. For whoever wishes to save his life will lose it, but whoever loses his life for my sake will save it'" (Luke 9.23-24).

A Living Lent [Day 2] *Friday*

╫

Led into the Wilderness

It is Friday of the first week of Lent. The Gospel lesson for the upcoming first Sunday of Lent is often taken from Luke 4.1-13. It is the story of Jesus' three temptations in the wilderness.[1]

It is very interesting that the word translated as Jesus was *"led"* into the wilderness can also mean *"snatched away."* This suddenness reflects our impulsive and instinctive experience with temptation. Since the word "sin" is such a slippery one in our culture, it is important to remember that sin simply means choosing that which does not lead to true happiness. Or, as Father Thomas Keating reminds us, "sin is looking for happiness in the wrong direction." Repentance, then means "changing the direction we are looking for happiness."

The swiftness of our own experiences of temptation feels like we are "snatched away." And in a sense we are, though probably not to a different physical location. The movement is within – almost as if our mind and soul shifts between windows running on a computer screen. Almost without our knowing it, the temptation screen pops up and we click it with our intention and will and we discover ourselves interiorly "snatched away" by thoughts, feelings or actions that do not lead us to true

---

[1] The account is also found in Matthew 4.1-11.

happiness or fulfill our deepest longings for communion with God or others.

Watching oneself in the midst of being tempted is hard to do. It is usually only after the fact that we can learn from our experience and see how it occurred. If one can begin to observe what is occurring within oneself in real time during the process of temptation one can begin to separate from the experience. In our interior, psychological separation or witnessing of the experience, a space for grace emerges and the Spirit of God will help us. The classic scripture for this process of dealing with what we have done and separating from its karmic power of shame, guilt and consequences is Psalm 51.1-14: *"Have mercy on me, O God, according to your steadfast love; according to your abundant mercy blot out my transgressions. Wash me thoroughly from my iniquity, and cleanse me from my sin. For I know my transgressions, and my sin is ever before me. Against you, you alone, have I sinned, and done what is evil in your sight..."*

If we are identified with the thought, feeling or behavior in the moment of temptation, it is like red wine pressed into a white tablecloth. We are totally absorbed by the feeling, thought or behavior. That's when we are most vulnerable. The process of observing and shedding our attention upon what it is that we are feeling, thinking or doing in that moment is a beginning step toward freedom. Observing a thought or feeling means that we are not it. And from that place of separation and observation, we can cry out to God for help. The classic scripture on this process is James 1.12-16:

"Blessed is anyone who endures temptation. Such a one has stood the test and will receive the crown of life

that the Lord has promised to those who love him. No one, when tempted, should say, "I am being tempted by God"; for God cannot be tempted by evil and he himself tempts no one. But one is tempted by one's own desire, being lured and enticed by it; then, when that desire has conceived, it gives birth to sin, and that sin, when it is fully grown, gives birth to death. Do not be deceived, my beloved."

The peculiar thing about sin and temptation is that it seems that we must experience it and indeed perhaps even fall down into sin and be snatched away in order to begin to understand its psychological and spiritual process in our lives. Once we have experienced the pendulum swing from desire, temptation, struggle and failure we will then accumulate a memory of experiences that can help us endure and not go along with future temptations. In fact, as one matures in Christ, we are transformed and our temptations change, even to the extent that what was once a powerful temptation in one's life, by God's grace and through inner growth, no longer is.

A Living Lent [Day 3] *Saturday*

A Jesus Lent

After months of waiting, it finally arrived in the mail. In August, I pre-ordered Volume 3 of Erasmo Leviva-Merikakis *Fire of Mercy, Heart of the World: Meditations on the Gospel According to Saint Matthew* and it arrived yesterday just in time for Lent. I had hoped it would include his commentary on Jesus' Passion, but it ends with Chapter 25, and in the Preface the author states that the present Vol. 3 grew so large that it became clear a 4th volume would be necessary, and will be forthcoming – so the anticipation continues.

I had the pleasure of discovering the writings of Mr. Leviva-Merikakis last summer. It was one of those providential encounters perusing a library, where I just alighted upon it as if it were wishing to be read. I picked it up and the opening chapters of his Vol. 1 commentary on Matthew absolutely stunned me by its beauty and interpretive depth.

As I sat in my study yesterday afternoon avoiding the Iowa winter wind-chill, leafing through this new Vol. 3, I knew I held a work of sheer devotion in my hands and gave thanks, welcoming it as an important companion for my Lenten journey.

The Preface greeted me right away with spiritual bread to satisfy my Lenten hunger. For example, this passage spoke to my heart in just the way I had been contemplating recently. Merikakis writes,

"Whether or not we will allow God full freedom to act in our lives very much depends on whether or not we will allow the total, unreduced, and uncensored figure of Jesus, exactly as portrayed in the Gospel, to approach and enter our consciousness and whole being. Hans Urs von Balthasar has commented incisively on the urgency of permitting God's Word to have its full way with us, unimpeded by either our innate small-mindedness or the pedantic strictures of our intellectual arrogance."

Theosis is a deeply important Christian theme that needs to be rediscovered by more Christians in the West, however it cannot be separated from Jesus. So that if you want to be transformed into Christ, you must follow the template of Jesus.

A Living Lent [Day 4]
The Frist Sunday of Lent

Into Wilderness

It is the first Sunday of Lent. A frequent Gospel reading for the first Sunday of Lent is Jesus' temptation in the wilderness. Today's reading is from the Gospel of Luke chapter 4 verses 1-13. This passage, also mirrored in Matthew 3.1-11, is one of my favorite scriptures because of its dramatic power and scripture based spirituality summarized by Jesus' phrase, repeated twice in response to temptation: "It is written."

I've found just the right book for the subject of wilderness. It is called *The Solace of Fierce Landscapes: Exploring Desert and Mountain Spirituality* by Belden C. Lane. Not only is Lane's beautiful prose, his is a deeply profound theology of place. He's writing about how our spiritual life can be shaped by our location and our relationship to the landscapes around us. Here are a few samples that blessed me as I reflected upon the Gospel reading for today:

- *"God cannot be had, the desert tradition affirms, if this means laying hold of God by way of concept, language, or experience. God is a desert, ultimately beyond human comprehension. John Cassian defined contemplative prayer as an imperfect yet "astonished gaze at God's ungraspable nature, something hidden" finally from human sight. Evagrius advised his students that "when you are praying, do not shape within your-self any image of the Deity." He knew that the God revealed in Jesus Christ is known ultimately only along the dry desert path of faith"* (Page 12).

- *"The desert makes it possible to learn the almost impossible: the joyful acceptance of our useless-ness"* (Page 23, quoting Dostoevsky's Ivan Il-lich).

- *"The significance of desert and mountain is not who resides here, but what we ourselves have left behind in coming"* (Page 24, quoting David Douglas).

Wilderness is uncomfortable for us not just be-cause it reveals our vulnerability to hostile elements and hungry wild creatures, but also because it reveals our self to our self. We can't hide in the vastness and we can't escape our thoughts in the silence.

The Lenten journey is an invitation to use this "wilderness" time of fasting to grow in self-understand-ing. Whether we live in a city of millions or a rural farm surrounded by no one but winter Owls, the interior wil-derness is calling; to be entered into, known and wel-comed.

Perhaps in the process we will also release our less real notions of God and enter more deeply into a stark honesty about who we are and how we are in relationship to Existence itself.

Remember, the first temptation for Jesus was a question of identity: who are you, really? The Devil, *diabalos*, is the divider. Literally, the "splitter" whose ideas intend to split us off from God and our True self, calling into doubt and question our true nature as being a child of God. Do not let the wilderness undo you. Nothing in the silence can nullify the Word of God, "this *is* my beloved son/daughter. "

A Living Lent [Day 5] *Monday*

✟

Centering through the Swings of Life

The Gospels present a mixture of emotions that occur in the short span between Christmas and Good Friday, a span during which we experience this Lenten Journey.

We are not well equipped for such emotional swings, but they are a certainty in this life on planet earth. That is one reason cultivating a contemplative prayer practice is so helpful and important. Meditative prayer has a way of balancing us, indeed centering us amidst whatever swings may be occurring.

Contemplative prayer is a receptive womb entered in the silence with consent to receive the Word of God as a bursting-forth-seed, bearing the fruits of Spirit – love, joy, peace, patience (to name a few) into and through our lives.

Experience, however, is not the ultimate basis of God's Word or Divine truth. The goal of the spiritual journey is not the death of Self after a blissful consolation from God or purgation in the wilderness – important as these events may be for our spiritual development. The goal of the spiritual journey is to realize and accept that there is no personal spiritual journey separate from the journey of Jesus the Christ. In one sense, there is only the journey of Jesus the Christ who, for us and our salvation, took the human journey on our behalf all the way down to "hell" so to lift it all the way up to "heaven."

All our journeys, however they may be going, are connected always and forever with Christ's journey. And this relationship of our journey to Christ's Journey makes all the difference in how our particular journey is going. Our particular journeys are held in the Universal Journey of Christ.

Everything that happens and occurs in this life-time, including the swings from joy to sorrow, is meant to lead us into a deeper and fuller relationship to and with the Trinity and transform us into Christ.

A Living Lent [Day 6] *Tuesday*

✝

A Faithful Fasting

Although we are just beginning our Lenten Journey, it is a good time to think about Easter Sunday morning; there is wisdom in beginning with the end in mind.

Perhaps the difficulty of fasting this Lent is lessened as we call to mind the joy and celebration awaiting each of us Easter morning.

This year, I wish to feel that I was faithful through the entirety of the Journey, not just in fits and starts. In past years, I have often gone slack in my intentions and lazy with my fasting, blurring the spiritual clarity that could have become a significant fruit of this barren season.

Perhaps that's a fairly normal experience. I don't think I'm the only one who finds that it is hard to remain steadfast, especially after the immediate Ash Wednesday enthusiasm wears off.

Remembering the joy that awaits on Easter, I wish for this Lent to be a faithful fasting. And I gain strength knowing others are making this similar wish.

A Living Lent [Day 7] *Wednesday*

✠

Something Greater Is Someone

A week ago we celebrated Ash Wednesday. The external ashen mark has long since washed away. Meanwhile the lectionary readings paired for today are Psalm 51 and Luke 11.29-32. The connecting theme is repentance. I'm intrigued by Jesus' teaching technique of comparison. He puts it this way: "*because of the preaching of Jonah they repented, and there is something greater than Jonah here.*"

Not so subtly, Jesus is reminding them of the prophetic repentive tradition and the means of grace that is available in the event of preaching. But there is something greater than exceptional preaching or even the kind of preaching that brings about a deep and an enduring repentance of life. That something greater is the living person of Jesus the Christ.

That is to say: as powerful and meaningful as your Lenten journey of fasting and repentance is, there is still something greater and more meaningful than any religious observance or practice. The greater part among us is the presence of the living Christ. How much more shall we be attentive to what God is doing for us in Christ than just our practices? It is a very subtle distinction that makes all the difference between a transformation of a life or a striving devotional religion.

But, you say, Jesus is no longer here with us like he was when he said "*something greater than Jonah is here."* For this, we turn to the Psalmist who cries out, *"create in me a clean heart, O God!"* And we are reminded of Jesus' teaching that, *"blessed are the pure in heart, for they shall see God"* (Matthew 5.8). True, Jesus the Christ is not with us in the same manner he was with the disciples in the first century. The sense-based apparent non-near proximity of Jesus' physical presence does not diminish the reality of Christ among us – by the Spirit, in the Eucharist, through the written Word of God, in prayer, in one another, in the least of these, in the silence, in the beauty of creation and from time to time in ecstatic visions.

The process of repentance is one of the means of grace that continues to make our heart clean and in so doing frees our perception to see beyond the senses into the zone of faith where God the Trinity pours forth love to and with humankind. A love that is more than just an energy field. The personal love, wisdom, power and presence of Christ is still available beyond Jesus' physical proximity or absence. It is an interior proximity, quite personal and up close experienced within each of our heart-mind-body temples.

Something greater than preaching or any spiritual practice including our fasting is still with us right now. That something is *someone*, the living Christ in you, known beyond knowing, felt beyond feeling, a reality of relationship possible for each of us through faith, which is the intimate and profound alliance between love and intuition. Repent. Be healed and cleansed. And receive the gift of transformation into Christ.

A Living Lent [Day 8] *Thursday*

╬

Why Lent

We know *what* Lent is (the difficult season before Easter) and we know *how* we do Lent (fasting), yet the *why* might be a little fuzzy. My Protestant friends might say "What's the point? We're saved by faith and grace alone?" My Roman Catholic friends might say, because that's what the church teaches. They might also talk about how the liturgical renewal movement has revived the season of Lent with sanctuaries filled in meaningful ways with barren trees and beautiful still-life scenes, tangible vignettes evoking the barrenness and longing of the season. But why?

There is no scriptural mandate for Lent. Just intimations, like the 40 days of wilderness fasting by Moses and Jesus prior to their significant teachings. So, why Lent?

Here is one aspect why: No matter one's theology or denominational disposition, human beings are spiritual creatures and we are created to long for God, even if we don't realize we are longing for God. Recall St. Augustine's grace infused autobiography that famously begins, "my heart is restless, O God, until it rests in Thee."

We need an annual Lenten journey because without an intentional practice of peeling away a little bit of everything else (except God) that we use to satisfy our spiritual longing, we'd probably not get the chance to see as clearly just how much our food, activity and money is used trying to satisfy our hidden and deepest longing of all – for God. We need Lent to show us ourselves. We need Lent to reset our system so to remember and return to God deeper in every dimension of our life. When this happens, we become a participant in the divine nature. We are filled with the freedom of holiness, the power of faith and the wisdom of love.

Why Lent? Simply put, yet profoundly experienced: because in Christ through this lifetime we can become more than just human beings. And Lent helps us in this life-long process. Interested?

One last thought. Friedrich Buechner once said that the 40 days of Lent is about a tenth of a year, so in a sense it is like tithing a tenth of our year to God. I like that idea very much. With a tenth offered, may God's grace multiply it one hundred fold.

A Living Lent [Day 9] *Friday*

⊩

Jesus is Who and Where, Christ is What

Today's Gospel reading (Matthew 16.13-19) brings us to the heart of Christianity – the recognition of and declaration that Jesus is the Christ. It is the heart of how we evolved beyond just monotheisim into the revelation and experience of the Trinity.

In this passage we are confronted with the meaning of this well-worn word, "Christ." The word "Christ" is the English translation of the Greek *christos.* And, the Greek word *christos* is an attempt to translate the Hebrew concept of Messiah, which means "Anointed One," which was a particular title. Beyond vocabulary, there was a historical meaning as well, as Israel hoped for the coming of its Anointed One, or the Christ, who would liberate them from their oppressors and lead them into a new season of blessings (See Jeremiah 23.5; Isaiah 11.2).

In contemplative circles it is common to fuse the word Christ with the concept of the *Logos*, which is the Greek word for "Word," as found in John 1.1-4, which famously begins," *In the beginning was the Word and the Word was with God and the Word was God*." Literally, we could read it like this: "In the beginning was the *Logos* and the *Logos* was with God and the *Logos* was God." I am convinced that without this passage of scripture the doctrine of the Trinity and the high Christology that developed at the subsequent church councils would never have emerged. Trinity and Christology need John 1.1-4.

The upshot for us is that Christ is a title, and therefore it is referring to something about the Being of Jesus. What might that be? Christ or Anointed One is a title describing the reality Jesus lived within – the union of human and divine natures. Human beings are born with one nature – a human nature. Jesus was born with two natures – a human and a divine. The Nicean formula puts it like this, "One being with two natures." Therefore, Christ is what Jesus was: the union of universal human nature with the divine nature of God (i.e. the *Logos*). Jesus is the physical, historical location and instrument where this union occurred as the revelation of the Trinity. Jesus is the Who and the Where. Christ is the What of this majestic and mysterious union; the union of divine nature with universal human nature. This union is what makes Jesus *the Christ* and not just Jesus of Nazareth. Thus, Christ equals the union of human nature and divine nature in the man Jesus.

This is more than just good theology. It is also good news for humankind. The good news of the Gospel includes the invitation that we can become "participants of the divine nature" (2 Peter 1.4).

This makes all the difference between just a "Jesus religion" where we reverence the historical person, and a "personal transformation journey" where our life is being united deeper and deeper, fuller and fuller into Christ; the life Jesus demonstrated and invites us into. St. Paul variously summarizes this process with his prayer for the Galatians that he is "*in labor pains until Christ is formed in you*" (Galatians 4.19).

Therefore, the continuation of the miracle of the incarnation can continue in us. That is why Jesus was born. Not just to keep the union of human and divine natures to himself, but to model the journey to us, so that our human nature is transformed into Christ.

As we abide in Christ and Christ in us (John 15.4), our human nature is transformed by the divine nature. Through our engrafting, our human nature is contacted by the Divine nature and begins to be healed, transformed and formed more into the Divine image, returning us to the Likeness of God. Another word for this is Theosis, which moves us through the process of sanctification to our destiny as Co-heirs with Christ (Romans 8.17).

So when the Apostle Peter perceives and declares that Jesus is the Christ, he is acknowledging that Jesus is the revelation of the union of human nature and divine nature. What Peter would come to discover is that this union can happen for us too. We are more than just believers in doctrinal information or news about what God did in Jesus or what Jesus did on the cross. We are more than *just believers*. We can become *participants in Christ, which is the unionizing process of uniting our human nature with the divine nature.*

Not only is the historical incarnation – or union of human and divine natures in Jesus – continuing in us as individuals who consent by faith to this interior relationship with God, the union of matter and divine presence is also occurring in the Eucharist, where bread and wine become the continuing presence of Christ by the spoken intention of Jesus. It is as if Jesus says, *this is really me. I am really present in and through these physical signs that not only point to my spiritual presence but also manifest it like a screen manifests or shows forth the movie projected by the source of light, which is the projector.* The spiritual and physical are interconnected, being transformed from one degree of glory to the next in a developmental, evolving journey into a future of Triune love.

A Living Lent [Day 10] *Saturday*

Deep Thoughts on the Logos Accompanied by Handel

As I write this, I'm listening to a vocal duet by Handel. It is beautiful and moves my heart to joy. It infuses me with a rare delight. It is the kind of music I need to reflect deeper upon the nature of the *Logos*. The kind of music I prefer to listen to on Saturday evenings. With sunset each Saturday, I conclude my preparations for Sunday worship. Quieting down. Listening to beautiful music. Reading. Writing.

If you wish to listen along as you read, here is the track info: *Duetto Per le porte del tormento (II, 8)* performed by Bejun Mehta, Freiburger Barockorchester, René Jacobs & Rosemary Joshua. The CD is Handel: *Ombra cara.*

With today's entry I hope to deepen my reflection that I began yesterday on the nature of Christ. Today, I hope to alert readers to some of the philosophical and spiritual rabbit trails I have experienced with the terms *Logos* and Christ. A warning. You'll need to read slowly. This is deep stuff, yet, of vital importance.

First, it is important to acknowledge that the *Logos* existed before the historical Jesus was born in Bethlehem. This may sound crazy, but it makes perfect sense since Jesus of Nazareth did not exist in history or in the flesh as the Christ (i.e., the perfect union of universal human nature and divine nature in one being) until *after*

[37]

the moment of Incarnation. This statement is only "fleshing out" the Gospel's insistence that "*In the beginning was the Logos and the Logos was with God and was God...All things came into being through this Logos...and the Logos became flesh.*" (John 1.1-4, 14). In theological circles, this is known as the *pre-existence of the Son.* So, who or what we mean by the word "Son" is a deeply important question. Is the Son the *Logos* or Jesus? This question led to intense theological discussion among the church fathers.

Second, in my view the pre-existent *Logos* is the "Son." They are, as best I can discern, theological synonyms. The *Logos* is the Son and the Son is the *Logos.* I can't go deeper into the nature of the pre-existent Son of God/*Logos* because that would get us into the inner life of the Trinity and that is beyond the scope of this Lenten reader, indeed, perhaps beyond the scope of my meditation at any time! However, if you are really interested I highly recommend reading the church Cappadocian father's on this subject; someone like Gregory of Nazianzus. Or of more recent theological vintage, Bernadette Robert's book *The Real Christ*.

Third, the pre-existent Son was *not* the historical Jesus of Nazareth *prior to Jesus' conception, birth and life*. The pre-existent Son *was* the *Logos,* the second "person" or energy of the Trinity. The incarnation is the event of the pre-existent Son or *Logos* taking on the form of human flesh and uniting itself to human nature. It is unfortunate the fathers chose the word Son to refer to the pre-existent *Logos* because it gives the impression that the second "person" of the Trinity is a masculine human, progeny to a masculine elderly man, called "Father."

There is no person in the Trinity. Nor is God three persons. God is beyond anything we can comprehend. God is God.

To put the point in orthodox theological terms: there was never a time when the Son, the Pre-existent *Logos (i.e.,* the divine Second Person of the Trinity) was not. However, there was a time when the historical, incarnated Jesus the Christ was not. When might that be? The simple answer is any time prior to when Jesus was born of a woman in Bethlehem in the reign of Cesar Augustus (Luke 2.1; Hebrews 1.1-2).

Fourth, the pre-existent *Logos* was united to and with universal human nature. In the event of the Incarnation – the historical miracle we celebrate at Christmas/Epiphany – this union was revealed to humankind. The human Jesus was the instrument of the divine revelation of the *Logos'* union with human nature.

In the event of the Incarnation something happened for humankind that can't be undone. God (*the Logos)* was united to universal human nature. Now, the two cannot ever be separated. This means that humankind is one with God (John 15). That is to say, in the Incarnation, a communion occurred for the purpose of re-creating humankind and transforming human nature little by little into the family of God as co-heirs with Christ. God came to us to take us into God. That is, in my view, the heart of the Good News of the Gospel. The church Father Irenaeus put it this way: he became like us so that we might become like him.

So, why is any of this important beyond theological circles of speculation?

First, it opens up a profound theological possibility for human oneness with God and keeps us humble in our view of other religions. Why? Because perhaps *the Logos* was active in other religious communities prior to the Incarnation. Who are we to limit what the *Logos* was doing? Perhaps God was building up developmentally to the crescendo moment of Incarnation? In fact, Scripture even hints that the Son/*Logos* was indeed active in other ways prior to the Incarnation. Just contemplate the meaning of Hebrews 1.1-4. Or try and wrap your head around the event of Melchizedek (Genesis 14.18).

Second, by understanding what actually happened in the event of the Incarnation and Ascension, we can begin to see why it is so important that we don't go down the rabbit hole of reverting back to pre-incarnational *Logos* theology/spirituality. It is very tempting and is, in my view, the ultimate basis and philosophical underpinning of some very popular contemporary Christian spirituality: the Christ without Jesus.

If you want the *Logos*, then you also get the revelation of the journey of Jesus. Post-Incarnation and post-Ascension the two can't be split apart. The wonderful result is that it keeps Christianity grounded in a living person – a relating, loving, divine-human being named Jesus the Christ who loves us, and is calling to us in personal ways to follow him into the heart of the Trinity.

It also keeps us in grace since God has already done what needs to be done for humankind. We don't need to rise up in consciousness or piety to obtain by our own efforts a certain "Christ consciousness." The invitation going forward is to become a *participant of the divine nature* (2 Peter 1.4). A participant is very different than a creator.

A Living Lent [Day 11]
The Second Sunday of Lent

Transfiguration into and by the Light

Today's Gospel reading (Luke 9.28-36) is the story of Jesus' transfiguration. It is a preview moment unveiling that there's more to Jesus than meets the eye. He's more than *just* a carpenter turned traveling inspirational teacher.

I'm writing at the close of this day of worship, aware that millions of people all around the globe today heard homilies and sermons on this scripture reading. If I had preached on this passage today, I would have shared a few of the following ideas.

First, the transfiguration moment is another occasion, perhaps the primary one, where we see an attempt to teach us what happens in the unitive state that Jesus lived in – the union of universal human nature and divine nature in one being. What I find most interesting is how the unitive state affects Jesus' physical form. It turns him more radiant, from the inside out.

How might this be? Physics can help us with this matter. If matter is energy and energy is matter sped up, or moving at a higher vibration we can begin to see not only how the transfiguration of Jesus' body happened, but also what Jesus' resurrection body was. The resurrection body was the full transformation of the physical form infused to the highest dimension of divine energy possible in human physical form, the first fruit of what awaits our own bodies.

No doubt there's a lot to this passage of scripture, especially the parallel to Moses' experience with God on Mt. Sinai, after which Moses' face was so radiant he needed to veil it to speak to his community (Exodus 34.35). But let's move on to a brief application for our lives.

Second, here is the connection for you and me. As we are united by faith in relationship to God, we become participants of the divine nature (2 Peter 1.4). This process begins to enlighten us and can transform our bodies and countenance from darkness to joy – literally, spiritually and physically. And the process of our transformation is possible because of our union with Christ by the power and presence of the Holy Spirit.

Third, the Holy Spirit is the connecting energy/person "linking" us to Christ and anoints and fills us with God's grace. It is important to know that it may not always be visible light, as it was for Jesus. We may feel it as a warming presence, which is also a synonym for love. Love is the warmth of God which we experience by the presence and action of the Holy Spirit. It may also be an inner light in a metaphorical sense referring to growth in wisdom or knowledge, insight or discernment, joy or peace.

Finally, the point I'm moving toward is this: the purpose of the divine mission of uniting divinity to humanity in the person of Jesus was not to keep it isolated to Jesus, but to release it by the Spirit and connect a large family into the powerful dimension of the unitive state available not just for Jesus but also now for and to you and me. This is the essence of salvation = transformation, theosis, divinization.

One clarification: whereas Jesus was born by nature in the unitive state as fully human and fully divine, we are re-born into the unitive state by grace, as our relationship to and with Jesus the Christ uplinks us deeper into a lifelong participation wherein we may absorb some of the Divine light, life and love.

From the Father's glorious radiance, Christ reflects to us by the Spirit – a glimmer of the full light of the world that dwelt among us, as us, revealing the mystery of the Trinity that is everlasting love pouring forth into the creation, and indeed creation's very source.

A Living Lent [Day 12] *Monday*

✠

A Martyrs Lent

I'm sitting in the chapel of the American Martyrs Retreat Center in Cedar Falls, Iowa. It is a quiet retreat center near my home that I enjoy getting away to for solitude and prayer.

As far as I can tell, there are only a few places dedicated to the remembrance of American martyrs. We tend to forget about them or not even know they exist. Yet, there was a time when this territory was on the edge of a vast forest and prairie wilderness. Unlike our civilized and comfortable life now in America, many of those first North American missionaries were martyr priests confronted with a profoundly daunting frontier that challenged their very survival. We owe them a great deal. So much of our comfort stands on their shoulders, as well as on the sufferings of the indigenous North Americans they tried to minster too and convert.

Today, there is not much wilderness left here – certainly nothing like there once was. But maybe there is still a dangerous wilderness lurking closer than I can imagine. In Lent I discover through fasting that an inner, untamed wildness exists within. It is just as vast and unpredictable. Just interior.

For example, it is humbling to discover just how primitive and seemingly threatened my life becomes when I deny it food, or its accustomed pleasures and treats.

Through this humiliation a gift is given: the gift of self-knowledge. I am discovering more about myself, and my sense of vulnerability. I am discovering how easily I give in to temptation, and how much I use food and other things to prop up my sense of safety, well-being and happiness.

I discover that I'm really not willing to die to myself, to food or entertainment, much less to die for the Lord as a martyr. Theoretically yes. In actuality, no.

I'm learning that Lent is the season of "martyrdom" of the little parts of my personality that function as independent fiefdoms avoiding God at all costs, and especially avoiding consenting more deeply to God's healing presence in the silence. It is so easy for me to do anything else *but* spend time in silent prayer and meditation. It is so easy to do anything *except* read scripture. It is so easy for me to go anywhere *but* to the prayer closet.

Surrounded by a cloud of martyrs who bear witness to the hidden life and the small, simple way of faith, I am edified by their courage amidst the temptations of life and culture to forget God for the sake of personal gain.

A Living Lent [Day 13] *Tuesday*

Wholeness Requires Uniqueness

The early morning light of this new day greets me with gentle snow, small flakes falling slowly. They say this will continue all day.

On Saturday morning, I sat in the silence of an evergreen forest in nearby Backbone State Park. The trees were still covered with snow and as the wind blew, it was as if it was raining white glistening flakes. The forest was shimmering as they cascaded down through the trees into the light and then back into the shade until they seemingly disappeared into the ground cover snow.

This provided an image of the spiritual journey we are all on. We are each like unique snowflakes emerging from the source (the sky) and our lifetime journey is represented by the path of descent (falling to the earth), and our death is represented by our addition to the snow-covered ground where there is no longer a seeming distinction between snowflakes – just the layers and layers of snow.

The piled snow is comprised of trillions of snow-flakes – each contributing their part. The snowflakes don't disappear into the ground they are united to it, inter-locking with other snowflakes like a chain of connections melted together.

I have discovered that Oneness doesn't require fusion of individuality. The Good News of the Gospel is that we don't just disappear back into the ocean, as separate and distinct waves who rise up for a moment and then disappear back into the ocean. That is not the Christian vision of our future. That vision may work within a pan-unitarian vision, but not within a Trinitarian, Christian vision where the resurrected Jesus Christ reveals the continuation of a unique being in relationship to the Father and others. Or, a vine abiding in the branch (John 14), oneness *and* twoness, which also becomes oneness and manyness. The image is one of co-relationship. Of inter-relationship, not absorption or dissolving into the void of God's infinite oneness. That is the vision of Advaita non-duality. It is not the vision of Trinitarian interelationality grounded in self-giving love. Christian Oneness is also Threeness and manyness. That is to say, relationality. And relationality requires unique beings in relationship becoming a community of being. Always, of course, with the caveat that God is not three beings. By "Being" we mean something more akin to Essence or Energy, or more properly indeed, three Revelations.

We do come from God and we do return to God. And in between we do learn how to be a unique being in relationship to and with God and other human beings. This relationality may endure beyond our death, as our souls and resurrection bodies await our full transformation into Christ and the Kingdom of God.

The Christian vision is becoming Christ by the Spirit as a co-munnion. A co-munity. An inter-relating-body of life in Christ comprised of parts that are not equal to the whole apart from the living One who is the ground and foundation, and indeed also our source-spring. Remember Jesus' words: today *you* will be with *me* in paradise.

A Living Lent [Day 14] *Wednesday*

⊞

Can You Drink the Chalice?

The theme today is removal. Let's pair the theme of removal with the Gospel reading for today from Matthew 20.17-28 where we hear Jesus say, *"Can you drink the chalice I am to drink?"* (Matt 20.22).

This question comes on the heels of a question posed to Jesus about who will be powerful when Jesus comes into his kingdom. The disciples were thinking Jesus would swoop into Jerusalem and take over as "President," and were wondering who would be his secretary of defense and secretary of state, so to speak. Jesus replies, *"You don't know what you are asking."*

If Jesus' close followers didn't understand his purpose, it is understandable that we won't either. So often it seems that the mindset of our world seeks to protect and prolong one's power at all costs. Rarely do we see the willingness to remove oneself from power or to *not* seek it out in the first place.

The comparison of the two ways is striking in this Gospel scene. Jesus' followers are thinking about their future possibilities and positions of power in a Jesus administration. Meanwhile, Jesus is thinking about his removal from this life symbolized by the drinking of the chalice.

There is a powerful thought. Jesus' power is the power of self-surrender. And that is the essence of Lent.

A Living Lent [Day 15] *Thursday*

Paradise or Purgation Redux

The Gospel lesson for today (Luke 16. 19-31) is a dialogue scene set in the netherworld where a rich man suffers in torment and a poor man in comfort. Sound unusual? It is a strange and wonderful parable, a real classic in Jesus' repertoire, for sure.

The phrase I'm interested in is the statement made by Abraham who is with the poor man in comfort, in response to a question asked by the rich man in torment. The rich man asks to be comforted and relieved a bit from his torment and Abraham replies: *"My child, remember that you received what was good during your lifetime while Lazarus [the poor man] received what was bad; but now he is comforted here, whereas you are tormented. Moreover, between us and you a great chasm is established to prevent anyone from crossing who might wish to go from our side to yours or from your side to ours."*

Perhaps the lectionary includes this scripture to encourage us in the midst of our Lenten fasts where we have given up what we normally would experience as good and comforting – such as food, treats or other pleasures so to focus our journey more on devotion to God. There is something to be gained through our giving up. There is something to be gained, sometimes imperceptible now, but later our fasts and little sufferings bear much fruit.

Perhaps also the lectionary includes this scripture to remind us that there is a chasm that separates. There is the possibility to experience "the outer darkness" and that this darkness is a zone of purification separated by a chasm from the comforts of paradise.

What might this chasm be? And please bear in mind that what follows is simply prayerful speculation. Since we are speaking of a profound mystery, let us do so with humility and love. And, with the recognition that all analogies are intrinsically limited in their capacity to explain in full, only in part.

So, with that said, perhaps a helpful analogy of what the chasm might be is the chasm of sleep. Sleep separates the realm of waking consciousness and the realm of death. It is an in-between state. It is not awake but it is alive. It is not death, but it is semi-conscious. In sleep we are not experiencing the fullness of life. So too with the chasm in the realm beyond this life. It is a transition zone mediating between two alternate realities: paradise or purgation.

Please notice I am not saying that death is sleep. I again remind you that I am *prayerfully speculating* that the chasm is analogous to sleep, that is to say, it is a transitional zone that is neither paradise nor purgation, but the zone in-between. As far as I can tell, we do not dwell in the chasm after we die. We journey through it. It might very well be the "tunnel" people report traveling through as they move toward a loving light in near death experiences.

It seems to me that when we die, we will dwell either in the zone of paradise or the zone of purgation. I deeply believe that because of Christ's descent into hell (which happened after his telling of this parable) there is the possibility for all human beings to be redeemed, to be rescued through the zone of purgation and brought to everlasting life. How could the eternally merciful one not keep the future open in love to the hopeful transformation of all souls from resistance to surrender?

That reminds me of something theologian Karl Rahner once said. In light of God's infinite love, you might believe in hell, but hell may be empty, or at the most populated with a few recalcitrant souls. In other words, no one is beyond God's power to heal and redeem, even from the depths of hell after death, or what feels like hell here on earth.

It seems to me that paradise and purgation are states of existence and consciousness, occurring *both* then and now. I know many find it difficult to believe or accept that there is a zone of purification or purgation after death. Since I have not yet died nor experienced a vision of this process I have no special knowledge on this subject. I defer to the tradition and to the church Fathers, who also are not in agreement on the matter. And I await my own death and surrender into the presence of Divine Love in Christ where I will know as I am known, trusting my continued sanctification to God's mercy and wisdom.

It does appear to me that there is good reason to understand that in the Presence of the Holy Triune One who is Pure Love, all that is in us that is false, resistant to love or self-centered will be purified away before we enter into the Kingdom of God. Perhaps this is similar to what Isaiah experienced when he was touched by the burning coal in the presence of the Thrice Fold Holy One (Isaiah 6. 1-8; 1 Peter 1.7). Who are we to know when the sanctification process is complete since we are not God? And why are we so certain dying completes our sanctification process?

From my own experience with the process of sanctification and purification of my soul-being, I intuit the process will continue after I die. Yes, I do understand that I am clothed with the righteousness of Christ, baptized and sealed with the promise of the Holy Spirit. An heir of Christ. All of that is true. But even still, I see that the process of sanctification continues, and has continued since the moment of my baptism.

Lastly, we are comforted amidst this speculation by Jesus' promise to the thief that "*today* you will be with me in paradise" (Luke 23.43), and St. Paul's reminder that "to be absent from the body is to present with the Lord" (2 Corinthians 5.8). Neither of these texts rule out a process of purgation prior to entering paradise, they simply assure us that paradise will be gained. And that is what matters in the end.

Perhaps also the lectionary reading for today is teaching us that Lent is a season of fasting so that the parts of us that are in need of healing and purgation might wake up from sleep and come into the light of Christ's healing presence. It is a time for us to be known as we are and to be transformed into who we might become.

Lent is the opportunity to avoid and lessen the time of purgation in the future, perhaps even beyond death. It is a time to become poor, not necessarily financially, but poor in spirit, poor in self, poor in self-will so that we might be rich in the Spirit, rich in Christ, rich in the Wisdom and Word of God.

A Living Lent [Day 16] *Friday*

╬

Life in Christ

God is calling each of us into a deeper fullness of peron-hood. Sin is our resistance to this fullness and also the rejection of other's fullness. When we reject another's becoming, or even our own becoming, it means that we are seeing only according to "the flesh" (2 Corinthians 5.16-17); that is, to see only *one* part of a person, not the whole. There is always so much more to a human being.

Getting practical, lust is often a result of only seeing one part of a person, not their whole. In fact, when we lust after another person's image or body, we rarely know the person beyond the surface, or beyond one part that we are attracted to. One night stands occur, in many ways, because people don't want to, or know how to move beyond the surface and be known more in full rather than just in part. It is a fearful thing to truly be known and loved. To be loved fully is what we deeply long for, but often don't know how to get or give.

This is why we need help and what God is trying to do by inviting us into fullness of life. Such fullness is similar to what scripture calls our "life in Christ" (Philippians 1.21) enabled through a paradoxical surrender of our self.

Life in Christ occurs in this life, for sure – in Word, Sacrament, prayer, silence, relationships, service and nature, to name a few. Our life in Christ will also be perfected in the next (1 Corinthians 13.12). Since the corrupt cannot inherit incorruption (1 Corinthians 15.50), we seek in this life to live dead to the flesh and to be alive in Christ (Romans 5; Philippians 1.23). Therefore we cultivate in this life the faculties and senses necessary to experience the kingdom of God and the mysteries of God's presence that we are invited to share in, both in the future and right now (Matthew 6.33; Colossians 3.2; 3.16; Ephesians 6.11).

The purpose of this life and the time given to each of us on this planet is to prepare ourselves for the fullness of life in Christ through spiritual practices such as watchfulness, love of neighbor and praying without ceasing (Matthew 25. 1-13). The technical term for this process is sanctification and Theosis.

If this process is occurring right now in our own life, and in the life of others, it helps us extend grace to others who are in formation and transformation. We are all in process. We can be gentle with ourselves, and especially with our failings, recognizing that we are simply in the process of being healed and transformed into Christ, even if at this moment it feels like we are going nowhere.

In one sense, there really is nowhere to go, since we are already "in Christ." Yet what is going away is our self-inflation. By the grace of God, it is being replaced with a fuller presence of Christ, which is the process we spoke of in a previous daily reading in which I discussed the concept of theosis. Patience. Gentleness. Humility. Such are the fruits of recognizing we are held by God's grace as we grow deeper in the life of Christ.

A Living Lent [Day 17] *Saturday*

⊹

Turning Deeper into Lent

This morning as I write I'm listening to a beautiful aria duet by Monteverdi called *L'Incoronazione Di Poppea: Pur Ti Miro* from the CD. It is sunny and cold, near zero degrees. A blanket of snow covers the earth, even on this early March day.

Four weeks from today we will be in the grasp of one of the deepest mysteries of the Christian faith: Holy Saturday and what the Creed calls Jesus' "descent into hell."

Beginning tomorrow, I will use each day to focus on an aspect of the events recorded in the Gospel of John chapters 13-20. My focus will be on exploring the characters and themes of the Passion narrative through a contemplative lens. I'm going deeper, following the story closely, listening in the Lenten wilderness for the inner duet of Word and Silence. Please pray for my continued journey, and I will hold you, dear reader, in my heart.

With Jesus, we now turn deeper into the season of Lent, focusing our intention, returning to our Ash Wednesday aims and asking for God's grace in our fasting, weakness and increased care for the poor and needy. Where we have failed and given into temptation, we are met with Jesus' mercy and compassion, inviting us to continue on with his words, "you are forgiven, continue on." I speak from experience. I have failed much already this Lenten journey, and it has taught me much. My intentions are weak and my "flesh" is powerful and sneaky in its ability to get what it wants, despite my aims to fast. I'm grateful, for this too is useful in bearing the fruit of repentance and humility. Success is not my goal.

May God help us all not love our comforts so much we miss the fasting graces. Amen.

A Living Lent [Day 18]
The Third Sunday of Lent

Returning to the Source

As I mentioned yesterday, I'll use the remaining time of Lent and this daily essay to journey through The Gospel of John chapters 13-20. To use an analogy from flying, I hope to help us get our landing gear down before we land. By exploring the Passion story prior to Holy Week I hope to survey the territory so we might all experience Holy Week as deeply as possible. We begin with John 13.1-2: "*Now before the festival of the Passover, Jesus knew that his hour had come to depart from this world and go to the Father. Having loved his own who were in the world, he loved them to the end.*"

Holy Week begins with love. That's in part why we call it the Passion. It is all about love. Divine love for humankind. Holy Week begins in the context of a Jewish liturgical event, what we call the Passover. The Passion is all about the nature and fulfillment of worship.

And Holy Week also begins with a mission. But, in order to comprehend the mission, it helps to retell the story in light of our new understandings of the universe. Otherwise, it is hard for us to understand the nuances of the Gospel story.

When the text speaks of Jesus coming to this world and departing from this world and going to the Father, it raises the question for post-modern people who have seen images of the universe from the Hubble Telescope just what this might mean.

For many centuries, humankind believed in an "up there" God, beyond the clouds, somewhere in "heaven." People talk about this still using the phrase, "you better talk to the Big Man upstairs." Yet, with our new understanding of the expanding universe some 13.7 billion light years old, we begin to see the vast scale of just what we mean when we say "heaven" or "up there." Literally, the Hebrew word is plural: God created the *heavens* and the earth. And "up" is literally in every direction!

So, when the text says that Jesus came to planet earth and is leaving planet earth, it is revealing the reality of a "higher" or "deeper" dimension of existence, perhaps even in a parallel universe to ours. It is important to keep in mind that the universe is not God. While it is super-charged with a mental or spiritual substance that we "live and move and have our being in," the universe and all that is within it, is part of the creation, and therefore it comes forth from God, but is not strictly speaking God. It is a manifestation in relationship with and to God, but the universe is not the ultimate reality that we call God, who remains always the Unmanifest One in Three: pure love, wisdom, intelligence and creative power sustaining all things.

God the "Father" is the source of the universe. Thus, Jesus is returning to a relationship, indeed the ultimate relationship, the relationship of Trinitarian love and communion, which is beyond comprehension to our human minds.

It is also important to remember that Jesus, as Jesus the historical person of Nazareth, had never before returned to the Father like he is about to. The reason is because Jesus was born on this planet. The Word or *Logos* in Jesus, the divine nature in him, had been with the Father before the beginning, and it is that divine nature or *Logos* which left the Father and came to join humankind as and in the person of Jesus. I've written about this in prior readings. The important aspect here is to realize that the return mission of Jesus the Christ back to the Father was the first ever mission of transforming human nature back to the dimension of the Father, wherever that might be.

While Jesus lived in the state of oneness in relationship with the Father on this planet, now he is preparing to experience the unitive state with the Father in a completely different dimension than what he was used to. And that is also what awaits us too.

To access this dimension fully, it appears that Jesus would need to die, receive the resurrection body and ascend to the Father. The resurrection body apparently transformed his physicality to such an extent that it became love, the primary energy holding the universe together. Composed of this "love" substance, the resurrected Jesus could move in and through the universe almost like light does.

Ascension could occur by means of what we now refer to as a "worm hole" or tear in the fabric of space and time, or more organically, an opening up to love itself like a flower opens to the sun. Jesus, who said he was the Door and the Way to the Father, clearly embodied that in his ascension and became the location where the door and way opened up for him to return to the dimension of un-mediated communion with God the Father.

A simple analogy might be this: Power in an outlet is the "Son." It is always connected to its source, which is the "Father." The energy between the two, connecting the two is the relationship we call the third person of the Trinity, the Spirit. So when the Son returns to the Father, the electricity leaves that particular location/outlet and recedes to its source. It will be fun to continue this analogy and introduce the Pentecost event, when the Son-life/energy returns by the Spirit to enliven us.

I leave it here, awash in the great mystery of existence in the vast sea of our universe held together by the field of love, singing its songs in the silence and pulsing forth the homing message from the heart of the Father – *Abide with me, become my beloveds.*

A Living Lent [Day 19] *Monday*

Lessons from Judas

Today we consider Judas, famously remembered as the traitor par excellence (John 13.2). His story surely informs the famous Shakespearean template of Brutus to whom Shakespeare has Caesar infamously say, "And you, too, Brutus?" Similar in tone, is Jesus apparent encouragement to Judas: "*What you are going to do, do quickly*" (John 13.27).

The betrayal episode of Jesus by Judas is a study in the process of our own experience of temptation. If we can see that there is a part of us that plays the Judas role in our spiritual life we will begin to see the interior depth-reading of the story that is seeking to unveil the very human dimension of our own multiplicity – that is to say, we are not always in agreement with ourselves. We are often double minded, weak-minded and easily swayed by alternative temptations.

Someone had to play the Judas role in the Jesus story. Someone had to be the one to bear the responsibility of showing the capacity of human nature to live by an alternative agenda and plan than God's. And Judas played his part well.

Perhaps too well, because he became overly identified with what he had done. He was swamped with feelings of guilt and shame to such an extent that he could not get internal separation from the overwhelming feelings. And this over identification with shame and guilt drove him into the despair of suicide. He could not move from the depths of shame to the freedom of forgiveness through the journey of confession of sin and failure, which is the remedy to being overly identified with our very powerful feelings of shame and guilt.

Identification is like red wine spilled on a white table-cloth. The wine gets totally pressed into the fabric. Separation and healing begins by the process of cleansing which in the spiritual life begins with confession. Perhaps one application for our spiritual journey is to become more aware when we are being tempted and say to ourselves: *this feeling or desire, this mood or appetite IS NOT ME*. It is an energy or program running on my system, like a virus running on a hard drive. Here is the process: observing the feeling or thought and not-identifying with it by means of using one's words saying, *THIS fill in the blank IS NOT I. I AM A CHILD OF GOD*. To do this simple thing is a major step in the direction of true happiness and freedom.

In the case of Judas, we see the sad state of a human mind totally captured by the thoughts of temptation. Perhaps his thoughts were even somewhat logical – such as, "maybe this will save Jesus from himself and he'll get arrested before he gets himself or us into any more trouble."

Maybe Judas' very practical mind was trying to control the situation without trusting Jesus. Whatever the case may be, his identification with his own thoughts about Jesus versus Jesus' word about himself led him down the path of betrayal, and once the deed was done he apparently rejected the grace and forgiveness available to him – a grace and forgiveness he had so often heard his rabbi teach about.

Instead of just grieving his sin, he also despaired, and this led to his untimely end. Wouldn't it have been wonderful if the Gospel message of forgiveness could have been announced to Judas in the upper room post-resurrection? That would have been quite a beginning for the power of the Gospel message – a profound template of new beginnings.

We close with a key lesson and distinction: whereas Peter in his shame grieved and wept receiving forgiveness after his denial of Jesus, Judas, in contrast, in his shame despaired, spurning forgiveness and grace, taking his life into his own hands – a very unstable place for anyone much less for one not thinking straight, deeply grieved and ashamed.

A Living Lent [Day 20] *Tuesday*

⁜

The Towel of Christ

For the next few days we will focus on the foot washing scene set in John 13.4-17. On the surface, foot washing was a common cultural custom for first century Palestine. What is unique is that this activity was normally reserved for servants, slaves or women. Not often was it that a popular rabbi disrobed, knelt down to the ground and willingly cleaned his disciple's feet. Keep in mind, they all wore sandals and the roads weren't paved with asphalt – a few of the roads were paved with stones. Also, animals were walking around too. Perhaps you can see the pungent picture we're stepping into.

The towel Jesus wrapped around himself symbolizes his role as servant to humankind, and more than symbolize, it is an entering into the state of all who give of their lives serving others. I think especially of the dear ones who clean up after travelers in hotels or the dear ones who clean up after our meals at restaurants, or all the ones who clean up our bathrooms at work or home. Jesus is entering into the humble role of servant, joining the ones who serve often unnoticed behind the scenes.

The towel wrapped around Jesus reminds us of his birth and pre-figures his death. In his birth, he is wrapped in swaddling clothes. And in his death, he is wrapped in burial linen. Jesus was a servant. He came in humility to seek and to serve humankind not as a power-broker of influence, but as an influence of power that brought healing, life and transformation.

Notice also that Jesus dries the disciples with the towel wrapped around him. Here we see the close association of Jesus as the one who cleanses and heals. The towel still wrapped around Jesus is an extension of Jesus and shows us that Jesus is taking onto himself the "uncleanliness" of his friends, removing from them that which would supposedly separate them from God, and taking it upon his own body. This too pre-figures a view of what was happening through Jesus' surrender on the cross: taking the sins of the world upon himself to cleanse human nature from the karma of our ignorance, shame and disobedience.

A Living Lent [Day 21] *Wednesday*

✜

Understanding Understanding

The disciple Peter's initial skepticism and resistance to Jesus' foot washing offer is understandable (John 13.6-11). What student wants one's teacher washing one's feet? It seems out-of-order, especially then.

Jesus' response to Peter is revealing about the level of consciousness (i.e. lens) Jesus perceives reality through, and his perception of the spiritual journey. The values of Jesus are indeed upside down in contrast to what our culture protects as the established hierarchy of who serves who.

It is as if Jesus says, "You only say that Peter because you don't understand what I am and what I am doing. But later, you will understand. Later you will understand that the nature of love is to serve."

Understanding. It is a pearl of great price in the pantheon of spiritual gifts. Jesus' statement gives us understanding about understanding. It reveals the developmental nature of understanding. Understanding, like faith, can begin as a small a seed and grow into something fuller and more complete. The key is accepting that there is more for us to understand. Our level of understanding, our depth of understanding, our scope of understanding can grow.

Understanding is also similar to wisdom. Whereas wisdom gives practical insight into complicated matters or decisions, perhaps even guiding one to the best choice possible in a matter or relationship, understanding is the sum total of our knowledge and Being added together.

One can have a lot of knowledge, practical or esoteric, and still be quite undeveloped in one's level of Being or spiritual maturity. Knowledge alone can simply puff up. One can also have a high level of Being, but not have much knowledge.

By "level of being" I mean the quality of one's being as a result of a deeper experience in God that has replaced increasing dimensions of the self with increasing energies of the presence of God.

When we grow in knowledge *and* Being we grow in understanding. Understanding is the sum total of the union of knowledge and Being. Thus, Peter did not have the kind of understanding to perceive the inner meaning of Jesus' foot washing. But Jesus promises that he will – later. We discover here that time is a factor in our development and growth in understanding; therefore make the most of your time. We may not understand something now, but we will in the future if we give ourselves to the process of growth in Christ.

By the time Peter was an elderly man leading the Jerusalem church, it is clear he obtained the understanding Jesus was speaking of. He writes: "So humble yourselves under the mighty hand of God, that God may exalt you in due time" (1 Peter 5.6). And here I take humility as the path of growth in being whereby God develops us, lifts us up in our level of understanding.

Normally, the higher level of understanding is incomprehensible to the lower level of understanding. A father understands his child's behavior because he once was a child. A child does not understand his father's behavior because he has never been a father. Only time, growth and development will deepen the child's understanding – often at great cost and difficult life lessons.

This is why we need teachers. They speed the process of our own growth of understanding, perhaps shaving years off our own efforts and growth and seeking. Teachers bring us up to their own level of understanding and, if we are so gifted, willing and wish to, help us surpass them in their knowledge.

A Living Lent [Day 22] *Thursday*

Leaning Back in Lent

"One of his disciples, the one whom Jesus loved, was reclining at Jesus' side. So Simon Peter nodded to him to find out whom he meant. He leaned back against Jesus' chest and said to him, 'Master, who is it?' Jesus answered, 'It is the one to whom I hand the morsel after I have dipped it.'" - Luke 13.23-26

During this Passover discussion, a troubling declaration is made by Jesus. He says that one among them will betray him. The disciples can't imagine who that could be or why.

What captures my attention about this scene is what happens next (Luke 13.23-25). The disciple John leaned back against Jesus' chest, perhaps his heart region, drawing close to Jesus and whispered a question to his Master: "Who Lord? Who is going to betray you?"

Jesus gives him a sign to watch for, and then enacts that almost sacramental seal and act dipping the bread into the cup and giving it to Judas initiating him into his work of betrayal.

What speaks to me about this scene is John's activity of leaning back against Jesus' heart or chest region as a symbolic gesture of inquiry into the meaning of Jesus' words and teaching, in contrast to Judas' departing from the table of Jesus: leaning in versus sneaking away.

Leaning into the heart of Jesus is still a possibility for us today. While not in the physical sense that it was for the disciple John, it becomes a spiritual presence as we lean into silence and solitude to hear the word of Jesus spoken into our hearts. Sometimes it is not even a spoken word. Sometimes it is just an interior impression or intuitive nudge. Sometimes it is a passage of scripture that rises to mind with power and clarity. Or perhaps sometimes it is the beauty of nature, or the distant bird song that assures you again the Lord is near.

When Judas left he was not only leaving the warmth of the dinner fellowship, he was also entering into the night, the ultimate symbol of what happens to us when we are disconnected from the loving heart of Jesus. The text abruptly says, "So he took the morsel and left at once. And it was night" (Luke 13.30). Night is the zone of sleep and darkness where we often forget who we are and disappear into dreams, sometimes even nightmares, and that is what Judas is about to experience. The nightmare of abandoning Christ.

The disciple John never did. He stayed beside Jesus through it all, even until that very heart he leaned into was pierced by the centurion's sword.

A Living Lent [Day 23] *Friday*

╫

The Way of Love

We come to the end of our reflection on John chapter 13, arriving face to face with several very famous sayings of Jesus. What might they mean for us today?

"I will be with you only a little while longer." - John 13.33a

The physical presence of our Lord and Savior Jesus Christ is normally not available to Christians today as it was for the disciples. Jesus is alerting us to the inner dimension that will be necessary for us to cultivate. Of course the context of the passage reveals that Jesus is referring to his imminent arrest and crucifixion.

But in light of his ascension, Jesus is also making a theological declaration: I will not remain on planet earth in the mode I have for these last thirty-three years or so. Christ will now be present to you by means of spiritual realities, such as prayer, Eucharist and preaching. Visions and appearances will occur, but they will be the exception rather than the rule. Nevertheless, we are urged to pray for Jesus' re-appearing, with the words, "Come Lord Jesus."

The early Christians began to realize that the sense of Jesus' absence was actually a presence. In the silence and solitude of places like the Sinai desert and the Cappadocia Mountains, Christians retreated to experience a deeper communion with the living Christ through their silent prayer and seasons of fasting. Perhaps, too, the initial absence of Jesus helped nurture the deeper understanding of the presence of Christ in the Eucharist.

Much of Christian practice and spirituality is a result of Jesus' words coming true: he is no longer here in the way he was, and they made their adjustments, trusting in faith that by the Spirit in Word and Sacrament the Lord was also very near.

"Where I go you cannot come." - John 13.33b

Jesus was alerting us to the fact that the dimension of his future existence is in the realm of the Father and this is not usually open to us in this lifetime on planet earth. Whereas Jesus lived in conscious oneness with the Father during his lifetime, he now was returning to the unmediated presence of the Father, which would require a resurrected and ascended body – something we humans normally don't have. There is a time when we will be able to go where Jesus went. And that time will come for each of us at the moment of our death. Until then we can grow in intimacy and oneness with the Father through Christ.

In fact, much of the rest of the Gospel of John, chapters 14 - 17 are dealing with Jesus' words of comfort and instruction in light of the fact that he knows that there is a physical departure of his presence required. Everything he says and teaches them from this point forward in the Gospel of John is meant to help them transition from his physical presence to his spiritual presence, hence the themes of the Spirit coming and his urging them to remain in him by loving one another.

"I give you a new commandment: love one another." John - 13.34a)

With this, we see the climax of Jesus teaching ministry. The consummation of his love and wisdom is the invitation to his disciples to experience the Triune life of love he experiences in and through the Father by the Spirit. This is the essence of the Johannine perspective: Jesus' experience of divine love that we are invited into. This perspective of love is unique to John, and perhaps is a result of his leaning back upon the chest of Jesus where John could truly hear his master's heartbeat and understand the vision of love that the Son was calling us into. It is this quality of love by which "all will know that you are my disciples, love one another" (13.34b).

We are still moving toward the embodiment of this love. The church needs to cultivate this interior union with Christ so to manifest deeper love toward one another. We are invited to move beyond the divisions so typical at the rational-egoic, and mythic-membership levels of consciousness and transcend them into the deeper, more mature experiences of union with Christ, which tends to neutralize every difference by the power of what I can best express and describe as a love-mysticism with the Beloved who captures our full attention more so than anything that might divide or distract us.

Focus on the resurrected Jesus Christ and his love will be enough, for his love precedes and supersedes all ways of being – even those you might disagree with.

"You cannot follow me now, though you will follow me later." - John 13.36

Now we come to Peter. And it gets personal. Again, Peter presumes something, just as he did on the mount of transfiguration. His presumption is misguided. No, he cannot attend to Jesus on this particular journey. But, later, yes. Indeed, Peter will also be arrested and crucified, perhaps even as tradition teaches – upside down on a cross. What I perceive Jesus to be saying here to Peter is fleshed out in Chapter 14. It is as if Jesus is saying, *"You will follow me later to the Father, since that is where I am going."* This has less to do with Jesus assuring Peter of a difficult death, and more to do with the assurance that Peter too will enter into the divine presence of the Father through the Jesus Way that is about to open up.

"You will deny me three times." John -13.38

Grace abounds. Just so you know you can't do this on your own. Grace abounds. Just so you know that you will not master the spiritual journey, grace abounds. The scathing honesty and simple frankness Jesus offers Peter with these six words about three denials is profound. There is no anger registered. Just truth. You are human, Peter. You are thoroughly going to be yourself, even now, when I perhaps need you the most.

Nevertheless, I love you and you will see just how much too. It will require your heart remaining open even when shame tries to make you close it the most. No Peter, there is an order to the process: first, you must realize how much you need the love of the Father and the forgiveness of the Son. Then, in the silence of your surrender I will meet you with the word of grace and empowerment. Peter, first I must suffer and first you must deny me three times. I wonder which hurt our Lord most?

A Living Lent [Day 24] *Saturday*

Un-Minding, the Way Opens

Our reflection for today brings us to the beautiful teaching hidden within John chapter 14. The entire section from John chapter 14 through John chapter 17 may be some of the most beautiful spiritual teaching ever recorded in human history, so meaningful it is worthy of memorization. Let us see what these opening verses have in store for us today on our Lenten Journey.

"Do not let your hearts be troubled." - John 14.1

Here is our Lord on the cusp of his arrest, trial and death encouraging his friends to not be troubled! If there was ever a time to be troubled would it not be *now*? Jesus' awareness of being in the center of divine order is clearly evident by his counsel. It is as if Jesus is saying, *"There is no need to be troubled when I am with you."* The Lord could say this because a union with the Father was at the center of his experience and his heart was not troubled. Later perhaps, his spirit would grow troubled, and at the end, he might even despair the sense of the Father's absence. And yet all of this was a part of the divine order of Jesus' journey, all the way into the depths of human alienation from God so to lift us all the way back to the Divine Oneness.

The word "heart" is a symbolic way of speaking of the whole person. It is as if he saying: "Let the center of your being, your wholeness, be at peace." It also is a reminder that we are more than our thinking heads, where we often get stuck trying to figure things out and untie knots that life has a way of tying very tight.

When we give up trying, and start un-minding we just might discover we are more than our minds, despite the enlightenment credo that "I think therefore I am." Perhaps that was appropriate for Descartes and human development at that time. But sometimes we can go too far with our minding and thinking. However, Jesus didn't say, stop thinking. He said: "don't let your hearts be troubled." It is as if Jesus is still saying: *It is fair to have thoughts and feelings of fear, but don't be undone by these thoughts or feelings. Don't live as if you never met me; as if I wasn't ever here. Let my presence and teachings guide and remind you so that you aren't ever again so vulnerable to the passing tides of your mind and emotions. Stay with me and I will stay with you. I am your Center now and all will be well.*

Christ knows that the way we relate to him is through our heart region, indefinably beyond our thoughts. When we are at peace in our hearts relating to Christ, all indeed will be well. Jesus was calling to his disciples to a level of love and trust as they entered into the new experience of his physical absence. He still is calling.

"I am the way, and the truth and the life." - John 14.6a

These GPS instructions are what Jesus offers in response to the question "how do we get to where you are going, Lord?" The message is clear. The way is through *me*. The way is through a relationship with me. The way is primary because it is a foundational relationship upon which to build a life. The way is relational. I in you; you in me. From this relationality springs forth truth and life. The inner relationship available with the Father through Christ by the Spirit bears the fruit of truth and life. Another way of saying this is that the relationship, the *way-ness*, bears wisdom and vitality for living life. People spend a lifetime looking for a way. We spend a lot of time and effort searching for the truth; and certainly tons of money trying to preserve our life and youthful vitality. Jesus is teaching us to let it go. He is inviting us to give up our peripheral pursuits and enter into a primary relationship with him and let Christ be our way, truth and life. And everything else will be taken care of.

As this process of transfusion occurs – our life into Christ – it doesn't mean that we disappear or lose everything we own; it means that our relationship to our other ways, other truths and other lives are transformed. They are set in divine order and arranged in such a way that they support our deepest relationship with God who becomes for us our primary Way. God becomes our center and from this place of centeredness we are empowered to live in the world with a joyful wisdom and a creative energy that knows it is secure, held as we grow deeper into our destiny as heirs with Christ, undeniably alive.

"No one comes to the Father except through me." - John 14.6b

Among the many things Jesus has said this is perhaps one of the most enduring and profound, albeit often abused. This statement is like love poetry and should never be used as an excuse to be abusive or rude to someone of a different faith. This statement is like eavesdropping in on the deepest bedroom intimacy of beloveds. The love of the Ever-Lasting Source who has Manifested in Love the Manifest Realms of the *Logos*, the Second Energy of the Trinity, was revealed in the Person of Jesus of Nazareth. Put that way *of course* there is no other way to experience the welcome home of the Father! There is no other way to a relationship with and in the Unmanifest Source whom we call the Father other than the Manifested *Logos* whom we call the Son now made particular on the stage of human history in the person of Jesus of Nazareth.

Put in the positive, anyone who comes to the father does so in and through Christ. By analogy, it is as if Jesus is saying anyone who is breathing, does so through oxygen – and Christ is that oxygen. Christ is the relationship that makes it possible for mere human beings to return to the Ever Living Almighty Source of Everything and not disintegrate into a pulp of clay dust in the process.

Here is another analogy to help us see what is going on in this statement. Perhaps if Christianity doesn't move beyond its more immature, abusive exclusivist interpretations, soon vast swaths of present and future generations will deem the beautiful Jesus' message irrelevant. Why? Perhaps because they can feel the fear and control and arrogance underlying the words and ideas that miss the essential message by thinking about it in exclusive human terms, not with infinite divine perspective.

Fear, control and arrogance have nothing to do with the message of Jesus or the possibility of becoming Christ. God needs nothing – no thing! No souls, no money, no nations saved. God needs nothing. God only loves, gives and creates. God is the fullness of fullness whose overflow is what we are and what exists as the universe. We are nothing and yet we are loved and invited to become participants of the divine nature, not manipulate the message for the sake of our little "Christian" empire building projects. So, here is another analogy to help:

Imagine the first plant ever that became green by photosynthesis. Imagine what it would be like for that plant to try to describe its relationship to the sun. Imagine if the plant wished for other plants to also get in on the process of turning green. What would the plant say? It would say – the only way to turn green [i.e. have a relationship with God] is through opening up and receiving the light of the sun [i.e. through the *Logos*]. Jesus is the first plant who is the first-born among a large family. He is the way. He shows us the way to be in relationship with God. We don't have to do what he did. We just get to follow Jesus' Way, which, in Christ, will take us to the "Father." In this way, we don't have to figure out how to "turn ourselves green." We just need to abide in Christ, as a branch abides in the vine – and let the vine take care of the rest of our transformation into abundant living life.

A Living Lent [Day 25]
The Fourth Sunday of Lent

The Spiritual Physics of Wholeness

"Believe me that I am in the Father and the Father is in me." - John 14.11

While the unitive state of oneness with God is described succinctly by Jesus, it is not easily understood by others. It is hard to intellectually comprehend such a statement like, "I am in the Father and the Father is in me." To begin, let's review a little of what I call the new spiritual physics: at the quantum level, quanta are described as the smallest known form of matter: 10,000 to 10,000,000 times smaller than the smallest atom. At that level, matter and energy are virtually indistinguishable. Matter is also not in a fixed "solid" state that we normally think of as "physical matter," such as a body or a desk. Indeed, our physical body is composed of "perichoretic energy," which means dancing energy. It is as if subatomic molecules are coming in and out of existence with desire or tendencies toward being and relationality toward each other; one might even say love is drawing them into existence and relationship.

Physicist David Bohm in his book *Wholeness and the Implicate Order* envisions that reality is an unbroken wholeness, and that any one element or thing contains within itself the totality of the universe. Physicist Neils

Bohr also suggests that we are in a relationship to this implicate order of wholeness, and that what we experience is not external reality, but our interaction with it. This is similar to the unitive perspective that spiritual teachers and mystics have been describing for thousands of years prior to the new physics in the wake of Einstein and others.

In light of these fantastic insights from physics, let's return again to Jesus' statement of implicate order and wholeness: *I am in my Father and my Father is in me.* By way of analogy, it is as if a wave rises up from the sea and then returns. There is no separation of relationship; the whole (ocean, i.e. Father) contains the part (wave, i.e. Jesus) and the part contains the whole. They co-indwell. The part does not contain the totality of the ocean, but the exact imprint of the ocean to such an intensity that the closer one gets one cannot tell where the ocean ends and the wave begins, or where the wave ends and the ocean begins. The two are one in a perichoretic dance of energy that theologians call loving communion – the perichoretic movement of energies between the Father and Son.

If that is what God is like, it is no wonder that nature reflects the image of its creator and source. Of course nature would bear this imprint! Jesus came to show us what it (that is, the implicate wholeness in relationship) looks like in human form. What's even more extraordinary about this relational foundation is that Jesus will invite us into the wholeness (later on in his upper room conversation). Here is a preview: "*abide in me, as I abide in you*" (John 15.4). This is so much more than theoretical spirituality. This is actually the formula to participate in the deepest level of ultimate reality which is the love and life of the Trinity.

When we do, it transforms everything and words become a means for participating in reality not as victims but as co-creators. No wonder Jesus could offer with such confidence the invitation to, "ask for whatever you request in my name (in relationship with me), and I will do it" (John 14.13-14). This is also the inner logic behind the Eucharistic declaration, "This is my body. This is my blood." In a world of relationality and implicate wholeness. The part is participating in the whole and the whole is participating in part by the attractive force of love and creative intention. Perhaps this explains also how Jesus' miracles were occurring. He was dwelling in infinite possibility and power (i.e. the Father), and infinite possibility and power were dwelling in him.

Recognizing this, reality became for Jesus on this planet "bendable" – reimagined by his creative intention spoken through his name. The result: a few fish become transformed into an endless meal. A big storm becomes calm. Deep water becomes a surface to walk on. Blindness becomes sight. On and on the reversals go until someone begins to wonder – who is this among us?

Perhaps you have seen the movie The Matrix. I think this presents one of the best visual descriptions of what I am trying to explain, albeit in a secular, non-theistic framework. Once you realize you are a part of the system you can step into and out of the system and even begin to re-imagine and re-order the system. Or, in the words of St. Paul, "*I can do all things through Christ*" (Philippians 4.13), which means, in Christ, through my relationship with the whole, I can do "*more than I can ask or imagine*" (Ephesians 3.21). This also explains why Jesus could seemingly promise so much to his disciples when he said: "*If you ask anything of me in my name, I will do it*" (John 14.14). Enjoy the wholeness!

A Living Lent [Day 26] *Monday*

Destiny and Development

"The Advocate, the Holy Spirit that the Father will send in my name – will teach you everything and remind you of all that I told you." - John 14.26

We will connect with this passage in a moment. First, a little groundwork to help us link up with the bigger picture of spiritual development.

Human beings are created for growth. We are designed to develop – physically, emotionally and intellectually. We also contain within us an Essence that some might call the Image of God, and others might call the Soul. Normally, this spiritual dimension of our Being integrates in a complementary way with our physical, emotional and intellectual capacities activating them to their full potential. This integration begins in early childhood infusing our normal human growth with something more than just a biological life. Unhampered, the process of integration will naturally unfold through each phase of human development leading to our unique flourishing.

It is apparently normal for that inner core of spiritual life and Essence to "seemingly" diminish as we get to the age of puberty. New energies arise in us and our interests divert from God, to girls or guys and for some, both. We seek to "find our place" in the world-culture and question who we are and what we should do and be. While we all may begin as little mystics, our personalities quickly discover more tangible interests.

One way of speaking about this process is that it is imperative in the childhood and adolescent phases of life to develop a very rich and alive personality that can, like a seed shell, encase the treasure of our Essence. The personality will serve us well from adolescence into adulthood. Indeed, it becomes our primary vehicle of interacting with life during this phase of development. Without it, we will not grow beyond childhood. Life and its vicissitudes may then hinder any further potential growth.

As we enter middle adulthood we begin to realize that the personality we have acquired – including our title, roles, relationships, knowledge, experiences, power, status, achievements, etc., does not ultimately meet our deepest felt needs. In fact, many times people feel that their entire lifetime of pursuits, successes and failures have let them down, or don't satisfy their deepest longings. Very often it is just then that a crisis of faith occurs – in oneself, in one's roles, in one's relationships, in one's purpose and even in God. This crisis is perfectly timed to help the shell of the personality, so carefully constructed over a period of twenty to thirty years, finally crack open, letting the inner Essence out, so to speak. It is actually not literally like that. There is never any leakage of Essence. Such crisis moments are risky opportunities. It is as if everything is on the line. One step in the wrong direction and we might teeter to disaster, breakdown or regress. One step in the right direction, and it is as if we move from hell to paradise.

While we don't really "crack open," perhaps this is what often does happen: the spiritual journey we are all on is designed to be more like nuclear fusion (by way of an inadequate analogy). The Essence is the "nuclear energy" and it begins to rise up in response to the softening of the personality by the blows of life so that the Essence energy can infuse further into and through the acquired personality. The process transforms the individual from the inside out by the power of one's connection to the Ground of Your Being, your Essence, your Soul-DNA, the Image of God in you.

While this process often comes to a more intense head during mid-life, it is a process that actually is occurring throughout every phase of our development. If you think of your lifetime as a deepening spiral, or as an opening spiral upward into God, each turn represents the process of disruption in service to a potential transformation. In fact, I have been with people in their journey into death who seem to "catch-up" in their development or return to repressions long ignored as they approach the end of their time in this physical dimension.

It is as if they are making up for lost time, and this seems to be a special grace of God's infinite love. It is just like God to not let one little lamb get lost in the outer darkness of recurrence or unresolved emotional energy. Such energies may impede one's journey into the next dimension. So grace urges us to make the most of our time and, as Jesus keenly taught, not be caught without a "wedding garment" for the "wedding feast" (Matthew 22.11-12), which is perhaps the event of meeting Christ on our journey from this life to the next.

So, connecting this to our text from John 14 noted above we can begin to see that the role of the Holy Spirit is normally not to deluge us in one moment of spiritual enlightenment with all the wisdom a person can possess, like downloading all of Wikipedia at once, but rather to journey with us and open us developmentally, phase by phase, into the deeper wisdom and love of God appropriate to our level of growth and understanding. There is indeed much more for us to know and experience; the Holy Spirit is the mode and environment in which we grow. And that is what a lifetime is for.

The Holy Spirit not only helps us along in our normal biological human development, the Holy Spirit can add to this process with the additional grace of enabling us to be born from above (John 3). The Spirit of God also crowns us with spiritual gifts and fruits that God promises to grace us with through our union with and in Christ. Such spiritual gifts and fruits are not contingent upon our personal development or natural abilities. They are graces. Perhaps they pair well with your normal disposition and personality; perhaps they surprise you and seem to come out of left field, "*I had no idea I could do that,*" giving you a certainty that God is truly the giver of every good gift.

Finally, it is important to feel the open-ended nature of the system. Knowledge of God is expanding. Revelation continues. The process is open. Jesus promises us the Holy Spirit who will teach us more than what we know right now. The Spirit is released to lead us further into the truth, deeper into the knowledge of God in Jesus Christ, a mystery that words fail to contain or circumscribe. And so we dance with our beloved in the still silence until we know as we are known, and our words are transformed into a wordless wonder. When this occurs, we will most certainly know this experience:

"On that day you will realize that I am in my Father and you are in me and I in you." - John 14.20

The destiny of our development and knowledge, and the aim of our Essence, is to receive and realize union with God through Christ as our continuous state of life. Not only know, but participate in this union of being. This is the purpose of our lifetime and this is the dream of the Spirit ever teaching, ever urging us onward into this most profound possibility of realization: *I am in my Father and you are in me and I in you.* May God aid us with grace on our Lenten journeys deeper into the heart of Triune love. Amen.

A Living Lent [Day 27] *Tuesday*

╫

The Sacred Place Inside

"Remain in me, as I remain in you. Just as a branch cannot bear fruit on its own unless it remains on the vine, so neither can you unless you remain in me. I am the vine, you are the branches. Whoever remains in me and I in him will bear much fruit, because without me you can do nothing." - John 15.4-5

On this Lenten Journey, I am focusing on what is known as Jesus' Upper Room Discourse (John 14-17) during his final Passover Meal with his friends and disciples before his Passion (John 18-19) and Resurrection (John 20). I'm doing this as a way of leading up to the Mountain of Calvary, fully aware of what has preceded so to be fully in the moment as Holy Week unfolds. This is a Lenten season of preparation and reflection.

Today, we come to this beautiful image within Jesus' teaching of abiding in relationship with him as a vine abides in the branch. There is so much that could be said about this passage, and reviewing the literature, most everything has already been said. So, beyond the meaningful "devotional" aspect of this passage, what might we learn about our own spiritual journey from this vine-branch analogy?

First, connecting with Belden Lane's insight below about how certain places allow us to experience God, I see the vine-branch analogy as indicating a place of meeting. A convergence. A thin place. See if you can detect the connection I'm hinting at.

In Belden Lane's magnificent book, *The Solace of Fierce Landscapes: Exploring Desert and Mountain Spirituality*, I came across a very profound paragraph. He's writing about the emergence of the *apophatic* tradition in Christian spirituality and what that might mean for our understanding of God's presence. Apophatic literally means *apo* = beyond, *phasis* = images: *beyond images*

"*It is impossible for human intelligence to comprehend God, yet certain places may allow people to experience the necessary risk that opens them, body and soul, to what their minds cannot entertain. God's places, in scripture and in the history of spirituality, are frequently fierce landscape settings like the storm-beaten slopes of Mount Sinai. God is 'an inaccessible and pathless mountain,' as Philo described the peak Moses ascended in fear and trembling. Such luminal places are able, symbolically if not physically, to put people on edge, driving them beyond all efforts to control reality (and even God) by means of the intellect...If we cannot know God's essence, we can stand in God's place – on the high mountain, in the lonely desert, at the point where terror gives way to wonder. Only there do we enter the abandonment, the agnosia, that is finally necessary for meeting God.*"*

On the mountain of Calvary there were beams of wood from a hewn tree. Here, is a place for meeting God. Here is the wooden trunk of Life extending its limbs for us. Connecting, we live. Surrendering, we bear fruit.

The place for meeting God is the interior nexus of our spirit with the Spirit of Christ. A union occurs, like the union Jesus spoke of occurring between a vine and a branch. It is difficult to tell just where the vine ends and the branch begins. It is not one, but also not two. It is a union, a relationship of mutual indwelling, I in you, you in me. This place is the holy of holies. It is where we meet God. You won't find this sacred meeting place in an MRI or Cat-Scan. It is not distinguishable that way. Perhaps at the quantum level, though, where there would be tracers left of the mystical communion of energetic Life pouring into our life at a cellular level – the mystery of being transformed little by little into the body of Christ.

You don't need to go anywhere or climb any sacred mountain or even be spiritually heroic in any way. We just get to "abide" in the interior relationship Christ continues to offer us by the Spirit in Word and Sacrament. As we abide, we are propelled into relationship with others in a new way. The way of love.

We carry the resemblance of the one in whom we abide, which is pure love, and this love begins to change us more and more into its image. Through the renewal of our minds, the purification of our hearts and the emptying of our self, we discover that there is indeed a non-geographical place of such vitality and abundance you might be tempted to call it Eden or Paradise. It is this interior place and experience Jesus was speaking of when he said *"the Kingdom of God is within you"* (Luke 17.21).

*Beldon Lane, *The Solace of Fierce Landscapes: Exploring Desert and Mountain Spirituality* (Oxford: Oxford University Press, 1998), 65.

A Living Lent [Day 28] *Wednesday*

✝

Serving into the Fullness of Joy

"This is my commandment: love one another as I love you. No one has greater love than this, to lay down one's life for one's friends." - John 15.12-13

Today, we look at Jesus' new commandment to love, and the quality of life this calls us to. Just prior to giving this "new commandment" Jesus reminds them that everything he is saying is so that their joy may be complete (13.11). While it is often hard to see, obedience brings joy. To obey, at heart, is to listen. Listening, especially as we get quiet in meditative prayer or prayerful reading of scripture will bear the fruit of joy in our hearts.

Thus, in one sense, joy is an important womb of Christian love for one another. Joy helps us to love one another, especially when it is not easy to do so. Joy helps us to consent to one another, and bear with one another in patience especially when we just want to do our own thing.

The phrase "lay down one's life" spoken in the shadow hours before the cross is a poignant presage to Jesus' own love for *these* friends that he is speaking to. It is important, however, to clarify just what Jesus is inviting us to do when he sets "laying down one's life for friends" as the greatest dimension of love.

In my view, this is in almost every case not an invitation to be the passive victim, or one who has no sense of self. No boundaries. No ego. Nor does it mean to die physically on behalf of others, as if in going into battle or taking the bullet for another. Such distinguished and sometimes tragic acts of valor are *not* likely what Jesus is speaking of here.

Jesus is teaching us that there is a kind of love that recognizes that the more we give, the more there is. As we surrender our own demands, needs and preferences, we discover that there is a joy and freedom in surrendering the thing we call our life; the thing we call my "Self." When we do surrender, we begin to realize that our true life is actually hidden with God in Christ and can't ever be lost or depleted. Many of Jesus' parables and teachings reveal this paradox of supply: wine into water, turning the other cheek, giving your jacket, the multiplication of the fish, the prodigal son's father, forgiving seventy times seven, the woman caught in adultery, the thief on the cross and the good Samaritan, to name a few.

This laying down is actually an emptying. Following Jesus' pattern, we consent to God's self-emptying process. In the process of emptying, over time, we are actually filled with Christ's spirit, word and love. The filling is possible because a space for grace has been prepared through the self-emptying, laying down process. Often times, the emptying process requires a humiliation, a contrite spirit. From this place of surrender, God's Spirit brings healing and hope. I always think of that special Cohen lyric: "there's a crack in everything, that's how the light gets in." Or out – in the realm of service.

Parents learn the gift of laying down their life for their children early on. Sleepless nights. Forsaking a personal task to play hide and seek, and countless other ways of living on behalf of the child's flourishing. Perhaps that is the best way to think of this invitation of love: to live on behalf of and for the sake of another's flourishing. It doesn't mean you physically die or go away to suffer, it means you too can get in on the joy of giving by being a participant in their flourishing. Notice carefully Jesus' words: "I have said this so that *my joy* may be in you and *your* joy may be complete." Surrendering for another is the kind of love that desires another's flourishing into fullness.

I mentioned above that joy is a womb, or context of Christian love. But there is another womb in which this love also comes to fruition. It is the context also of this passage of scripture, the context of Eucharist and Service. Jesus is serving his disciples in both the foot washing and institution of the first communion meal. So we see from the beginning that service and Eucharist go hand in hand (perhaps I should say go foot and hand).

You might be interested to know that Saint Benedict, founder of Western Monasticism, based his Rule on the fact that service flows out of the Eucharist. He draws attention to the special connection found also in the Gospel of Luke: *"Who is the greater: the one at table or the one who serves? The one at table, surely. Yet here am I among you as one who serves."* (Luke 22.27).

Service to one another is how we "lay our life down" for the sake of fellowship and community. It is counter cultural and counter intuitive. Who in power serves the powerless? In our world, isn't it the other way around?

During Lent we are invited to serve and love in practical ways, especially the poor, needy and sick, through increased acts of charity and almsgiving. What I find most beautiful is that this service of pouring our lives out for others is grounded in the Lord's Table, the Eucharist, wherein we hear the sacred words, "This is the cup of my blood…it will be shed for you and for all." We don't normally shed our blood in service, but we do spend our life energy, our life force – which our physical "blood" represents.

When we give of our Essence, it will bear fruit no matter what. When we serve others as a "pouring out" of our utmost attention and Being, it will come back to us perhaps even one hundred fold. One caution: we never do in order to get, nor give to receive. We do however honor the deep principle that: *you cannot out give Love*. The more you give, the more it gives because Divine love is constantly pouring out from the infinite abundance of the Triune God through Christ by the Spirit with the prayers of Mary and all the Saints in service to our flourishing and full joy in this life and the next.

A Living Lent [Day 29] *Thursday*

⳨

Wholeness and Multiplicity

"If the world hates you, realize that it hated me first." - John 15.18

The last section of John 15 verses 18-27 can be troubling. It seems Jesus is a bit on edge, and to some, over the top. One doesn't quite feel the love. Perhaps this is an overre-action on the part of Jesus, or stress, given the hour in his life. Regardless of your interpretation of these verses, there is an inner, contemplative way to read this passage as well that opens it up in what are, in my view, fruitful ways. Here is one:

The first thing we need to remember is that we are a multiplicity. There are many different voices and iden-tities within us. Most of us are not one solid I. We are a legion of dimensions and I's. While this is hard to some-times accept, it is easier to observe. Just notice the differ-ent ways you are in public and private. Our multiplicity also shows up as little negative, fragmented I's gang up into groups. These can sometimes become personality disorders or states of power that seem to take us over, such as rage or lust or addiction. One of the most difficult things to our sense of pride and sense of self is to admit that we are a multiplicity. I'll never forget talking with a drunk who the morning after a violent rampage said to me in tears, "but I'm not like that. That's not really me." "I know," I said, "It is just one part of you and that part can be forgiven and healed."

If we are a multiplicity, and if we approach this passage from the contemplative, inner dimension which places us within the text, then we can move to a place of seeing that Jesus is speaking of the "world" that is within us. Try this on:

The world represents those parts within us that are resistant to God's grace, that are negative, hateful and do not obey the word of God. These parts of us are the "They" Jesus speaks about. So, here is a little exercise. Read the passage and whenever you read these specific words "world," "they," "them," and "whoever" (in the New American Bible Version, at least), translate that as – "the I's in me, or the parts in me." By doing this, it opens this passage up to a whole new dimension. The bad guys aren't out there – they are also in me. There are parts of me that hate Christ. That hate the Father. That resist God's word and don't believe. In Paul's dualism, this is the multiplicity between our Flesh (i.e. the false self) and the Spirit (i.e. the true Self touched by Holy Spirit).

But there are also parts of me that do receive and believe and love Christ and the Father and God's word. These are the higher or deeper parts of my Self connected to my Essence, awakened by Grace, and led by the Spirit. The Advocate, who Jesus promises he will send, does come to our interior states and when this happens, again and again, it is as if we are saved from ourselves. Rescued and lifted up from negative, hateful states and I's that we're taking over our interior disposition and external expressions.

In time, through the sanctification process, our interior life increasingly becomes more solid and One. Our multiplicity dissipates and the random negative hateful little i's in us are neutralized and integrated like salt neutralizing spice. This brings new meaning, I think, to Paul's vision that it is "I, not I, Christ in me" (Galatians 2.21). Internal solidity through our union with Christ is a distinct and compelling possibility for our lifetime enabling our "yes's to be yes, and our no's to be no." It allows us to serve one master and obey the voice of the Lord. No wonder Jesus said, "A house divided against itself cannot stand." We are the house. And we are often divided amongst ourselves and multiplicity within, not to mention its various stories: upper, middle and lower, that is, mind, heart, body.

By the way, both disciples Peter and Judas are perfect examples of how the multiplicity plays out. Both had little fearful, negative I's in them that did not listen to the Spirit but followed their own advice leading to the less than ideal acts of betrayal and denial. We can have empathy because if we look closely, we can see these same I's in us, at least I find them in me all the time, which is why I am on this Lenten Journey, asking for my Teacher and Lord to heal me and make me whole, truly One in Christ.

A Living Lent [Day 30] *Friday*

╫

Uploaded into the Cloud

"It is to your advantage that I go away, for if I do not go away, the Advocate will not come to you; but if I go, I will send him to you." - John 16.7

As we enter into John chapter 16, we draw nearer to the end of Jesus' Upper Room Discourse, which concludes with what is known as Jesus' High Priestly prayer in John chapter 17.

In John chapter 16, we return to the theme begun in Chapter 14 about the Spirit that will soon be given as well as Jesus' imminent physical absence. Here, we see the need for Jesus' departure reiterated. Indeed, it is not just a need it is called an "advantage" to the disciples. What might this mean?

The Advantage of the Spirit is what I call the hinge of scripture. The transition to a Spirit based relationship of the church with God *from* the incarnate Jesus relationship is perhaps one of the most important aspects of Jesus' ministry. We tend to heavily emphasize Jesus' ministry, teachings, Cross and Resurrection, but de-emphasize the event of Pentecost, and the sending of the Holy Spirit, or the Spirit of Christ. They are essentially synonyms. Perhaps we de-emphasize because our minds can grasp the more concrete realities of the Jesus story, whereas it is more difficult for our sense-based thinking to grasp the Spirit. For many, the Spirit is like a distant

3rd cousin in the family, not the third person of the Trinity.

Here are a few analogies to help us see how important this event of the giving of the Holy Spirit is. By analogy, the "going away" of Jesus is like when you take your hands off your kid's bike as they are riding it. You must "go away" in order so that they might experience the fullness of riding a bike, which was the very purpose you bought them a bike. You gave the gift of a bike so that they too could participate in the experience of riding it. The point is that Jesus didn't just show up among us so that we would say, "Wow, what an amazing bike! He was a great bike rider!" So, we build a museum and put a statue of the bike and a great picture of Jesus' riding the bike down a lovely lane by the sea and then bow down to it. It is so much more than that: Jesus came so that he would "heal" the bike by riding it himself, and then invite us to ride it with the help from the "wind at our back," which is his Spirit. That is an external analogy and it only does partial justice to the spiritual dynamic involved. Here is another try.

A more realistic analogy comes from biology. In Jesus Christ we had a prototype genetic event. The prototype worked. Jesus was the splicing together of human and divine DNA, so to speak. In order for the prototype "splice" to be distributed and replicated to others, the host carrier, Jesus, will need to share the splicing but this will require a total transformation of his being (death, resurrection, glorification) and that through this glorification process, by the power and means of the "Spirit" the glorified Jesus can incorporate others into the life and wholeness obtained through the splicing event. The Spirit becomes the mode and environment by which the replication occurs.

I know this is challenging, so one final analogy, saving the best for last. I'm approaching this from several angles since this is important for our understanding and experience of a lived Christian spirituality.

Imagine that Jesus Christ is a song, a very beautiful symphony, that we can listen to and experience only if we are connected to the "audio" stream and receive the continuous download of the music from the iCloud. In this analogy, we each are the audio player device, Christ is the content saved in the Cloud (i.e. the music) and downloaded or streamed to us by an internet connection. Thus, the Holy Spirit is the connection between the device and the content, that is to say, the Spirit is the means by which we are receiving the music, receiving Christ (i.e. music) into our player (i.e. life). The Spirit is the go between that connects you and Christ in relationship, just like the internet is the go between connecting your computer or device to the music content in the cloud.

Going deeper with the analogy, imagine a composer writing a beautiful symphony, recording it and then saying, now, I'm just going to put this in my safe and only listen to it on special occasions, perhaps Christmas and Easter. That would be unfruitful for everyone, especially the composer. In this analogy, God the Father is the composer, Jesus the Christ is the composition and when the composition gets uploaded "ascended" into the Cloud, it is made available to be streamed to anyone with a device capable of receiving a download by the Spirit. If the connection is lost, the music stops. That is why we must not grieve the Spirit, for the Spirit is our connection to and with Christ.

The ultimate experience of this of course is with the Eucharist, where the host of bread and wine represent Christ, and the Spirit transforms it into the living presence of Christ to and for, and within all who partake.

A Living Lent [Day 31] *Saturday*

⧾

There Is More

"I still have many things to say to you, but you cannot bear them now. When the Spirit of truth comes, he will guide you into all the truth..." - John 16.12-13

The wisdom of the Holy Spirit, like God, is unending; at least from the perspective of a human being. In this passage, Jesus again reminds his disciples that there will be more to come after his departure. The Spirit will lead them deeper. His teaching was just the beginning. With that phrase, comes all the challenges of determining and defining just what is the Spirit's "more to come" teaching. Is this? Is that?

Orthodoxy, and the discernment of its presence, *is not* the subject of this reflection. What *is* the subject is Jesus' superabundant promise that we couldn't handle everything he could have said – it would have overwhelmed us. Here is a story and analogy to help make the connection with what Jesus is saying.

Antoine de Saint-Exupéry tells the story of taking a group of North African Bedouins to visit Europe. These desert nomads had spent their lifetimes sun-scorched and fiercely aware that life in the desert was an exercise of conservation and restraint. In the vast engulfing desert wasting any resource, especially the silver treasure of water was not only inconceivable; it was also life-threatening. Saint-Exupéry recounts that when the Bedouin's were shown the marvels of Western civilization such as the Eiffel Tower, locomotives and steamships, they were indifferent. But when they saw the glorious towering trees along the Seine River, and the nearby Parisian forests, the Arabs wept. They had never seen a tree, a waterfall, or a rose.

Author Belton Lane comments on this story that, "the only natural world they [the Bedouin's] had ever known was flagrantly stingy with its gifts. Years of desert attentiveness had trained them to expect only shortfall and subtlety. Back home, where water was precious, they might walk for days on end in search of a tiny spring, maybe a handful of palms. So when they stood in a high alpine meadow beside an enormous waterfall in the French Alps, its water roaring out of the mountain in a huge braided column, they had no way of comprehending such lavishness."*

Saint-Exupéry captures the moment: "They stood in silence. Mute, solemn...gazing at the unfolding of a ceremonial mystery. That which came roaring out of the belly of the mountain was life itself, was the life-blood of man. The flow of a single second would have resuscitated whole caravans that, mad with thirst, had pressed on into the eternity of salt lakes and mirages. Here God was manifesting Himself: It would not do to turn ones back on Him." The Bedouins refused to leave until the water stopped. They said it would be disrespectful to God. Their guides, knowing that the water would not cease said something which they knew would be incomprehensible to these desert pilgrims: "gentlemen, this water has been running like this for a thousand years!"**

Perhaps we have grown bored by our faith or religion. Or even of our Lenten Journey. Perhaps we have lost our sense of wonder, and long ago ceased to believe that there was anything more than just the endless circle of the liturgical year. Oh well, "it's Lent again. I'll just suffer through it till Easter."

Perhaps we have become too accustomed to the holy things amidst us, similar to the local alpine dwellers whose daily life with the roaring waterfall might lead them to live as if it weren't even there, until strangers from a foreign desert land arrive and remind them by their tears and awe just how much more there is to this dimension called life in Christ surrounding them – Christ, who is Living Water, poured out from an endless depth by the ever-present teacher that Jesus called "my Spirit."

*Beldon Lane, *The Solace of Fierce Landscapes* (Oxford: Oxford University Press, 1998) 203.
**Saint-Exupery, *Wind, Sand and Stars,* pp. 138 – 144.

A Living Lent [Day 32]
The Fifth Sunday of Lent

An Imperturbable Center

"In the world you face persecution. But take courage; I have conquered the world!" - John 16.33

John chapter 16 concludes repeating many of the previous themes highlighted in chapters 13-15, especially the fact that Jesus will be leaving the disciples soon. The final message before Jesus' prayer which begins in John chapter 17 is an evocative call to courage, despite the gloomy news that the disciples can count on future persecution. As Jesus mentioned earlier, a servant is not greater than the master. Thus, if the master-teacher was persecuted it follows that the servant-disciples will be too.

Again, we wish to make a contemplative turn and interpret this concept of persecution from the interior dimension. That is to say, to locate ourselves within the text *and* the text within ourselves. Thus, in addition to "the world" representing external forces such as criticism and judgment by governmental forces or cultural powerbrokers, you might also expect to discover that the contemplative perspective on this passage is that "the world" is within us – it represents the totality of our thoughts, emotions and physical experiences. These can be "the world," and they can often times persecute us; they can literally be against us.

The reason this is so is because we have a False Self and a True Self. In these categories, the False Self represents the interior world that persecutes. The True Self represents the interior dimension of peace, non-reactivity to negativity, and what might be best described as an imperturbable center. I'm not talking about stoicism; I'm talking about a God directed center that is not undone by whatever is occurring within or without.

From this place of centeredness, courage arises not because we are heroic, but because the centered life is mostly a fearless life since there is nothing to defend. One belongs to God and this physical existence is not the totality of one's life. And so, one is truly free to surrender, to give up everything since it is really no-thing in the first place. Jesus models this centered living despite what was happening in the external world around him. He was completely devoted to God's voice and vision for his life. That's not to say Jesus didn't ask questions or ponder if things could be different. In the end, he accepted that his life was hidden within God's and that he could entrust his deepest being, that is, his Spirit to Abba with a cry inspired by the imperturbable confidence of one who cried out: *not my will, but thy will be done.*

St. Paul spoke of this interior place of peace and courage as being the state of godliness with contentment, so that no matter what happens in the external situations of life, one can declare that "nothing can separate me from the love of God in Christ" (Romans 8.28-39). Our Lenten Journey teaches us to welcome and accept whatever is occurring, even if it might be external or internal persecutions from other people or our interior thoughts.

A Living Lent [Day 33] *Monday*

Lent**ernal** *Life*

"And this is eternal life, that they may know you, the only true God, and Jesus Christ whom you have sent." - John 17.3

A week from today we will be in Holy Week. Our Lenten Journey is nearing its conclusion. In preparation, we enter into Jesus' prayer as recorded in John chapter 17. The Gospel of John is my companion this Lent, helping me review the events prior to, during and following Jesus' Passion. In this passage, Jesus equates eternal life with knowledge of God and knowledge of himself. What might this mean for my Lenten Journey?

First, an important question. What is eternal life? The word for "eternal" can mean multiple things, including unending or overflowing. If you read it, as we so often do, in terms of a *quantity* of time, (i.e., unending time, eternal) then we often think of a future state of paradise after we die where we live on forever.

However, we can also read it as an unending *quality* of life. In that case, it might be more helpful to translate eternal life as "fullness of life" or "the ultimate purposeful life" or "deepest quality of life." This takes away the sole emphasis on the future escapism that has often accompanied preaching about eternal life. If eternal life is solely about time, than we can't really access it until we die. It also decreases the urgency of caring about this world and its ecosystems, since in the end, true, eternal life is waiting us in paradise. If this eternal life is also about quality of life here and now, then that opens up wonderful possibilities for engagement with the world and inspiration for our spiritual journey here and now, which in my view, makes a big difference.

Our Lenten Journey is an opportunity for us to experience the quality of this "fullness of life." I call it Lenternal Life. It is a cute way of remembering that there is more to being a Christian than waiting for heaven. There is more to believing in Jesus than just as a fire insurance policy protecting against eternal damnation.

Second, the fullness of life that is available through knowing God and Jesus the Christ is also pointing to the relational dimension of the spiritual life. The word "know" that Jesus uses recalls the Hebrew word used in the opening story of Genesis to describe the intimate communion of husband and wife – they *knew* one another, and a child was produced. That is to say, this knowing is not just intellectual. It is not just a knowing of a certain kind of information or even the right information, say like Jesus' name or that he died upon the cross. This knowing of God and Jesus the Christ would be better understood if we translated the phrase like this: *And this is the deepest, fullest life possible – a relationship with the Triune God through Christ by the Spirit.*

And such a relationship invites us into time and to cultivate the relationship through practices of devotion, such as centering prayer or the Jesus' prayer.

Perhaps such cultivation is what the Lenten Journey is all about. There is really no reason to wait for eternal life in heaven. Eternal life is also available right now in an interior relationship in Christ by the presence and power of the Spirit – no matter what is occurring in one's external day-to-day life of family, work and activities.

A Living Lent [Day 34] *Tuesday*

⊹

Centered Life

"Now they know that everything you have given me is from you; for the words that you gave to me I have given to them…" - John 17.7-8

By now, Jesus seems certain his disciples realize that *everything* he has done and taught is the fruit of his relationship with the Father, whom Jesus called Abba.

Despite Jesus' best attempts to establish this fact, it appears many of the disciples gave up on that idea in the hours immediately leading up to their teacher's death. When things go badly, from an external perspective, it is hard to see how God is present.

One of the lessons from this passage and the entire prayer given by Jesus in John 17 is that there is a center and source for all things. In the case of Jesus' spiritual life and wisdom that center and source was his relationship with Abba.

For us, we are now invited into a relationship with the center and source as well through Jesus. Everything has a center. Without a center things fall apart. What is yours?

As Jesus taught, you will know a tree by its fruit. Perhaps we can shift that saying and put it this way: you will know a person by their center. What is the center of your life? Around what do you orbit? What holds your life's attention?

Jesus invites us to a centered relationship with his Father through his living Word and Spirit. What that looks like in each of our lives today might be different, and yet there will be similar fruit – the increasing presence of love, joy, peace, patience and kindness, to name a few.

The Word of God, living and written, is our primary way of centering our life in Christ. So too is prayer, especially a meditative prayer method such as Centering Prayer. And certainly partaking frequently in the Eucharist, the Lord's Supper, as the physical embodiment of living in relationship to the Triune Center, Father, Son and Holy Spirit.

A Living Lent [Day 35] *Wednesday*

✝

Silent Oneness

"I ask not only on behalf of these, but also on behalf of those who will believe in me through their word, that they may all be one. As you, Father, are in me and I am in you, may they also be in us…" - John 17.20-21

On this first day of Spring, I am celebrating the Spring Equinox by listening to Aaron Kernis' *Symphony No.2 – Musica Celestis* (for string orchestra). I first heard it nearly a decade ago, live at the Detroit Symphony.

Today, as the sun meets the Northern hemisphere with equal light between day and night, I turn to the final verses of John chapter 17 to hear Jesus speak – as if gazing into the future, perhaps even perceiving this Lenten Spring day – not just to his disciples in that moment, but also to us. As he puts it, "to those who *will* believe…"

As I have contemplated this ending prayer of Jesus, it occurs to me to say as little as possible. What is on my heart is the wish for oneness among Christians. A oneness that Jesus could envision and request on our behalf. I contemplate why there has not been oneness. So much of our history as the church has been dividedness.

I just returned from a 10 day centering prayer retreat. We are silent for 9 days with virtual strangers, sitting in a prayer circle for up to 4 hours a day. We don't speak or share our personal stories. And yet at the end of the retreat a sense of oneness and intimacy has grown through the silence. I often marvel how without speaking to one another somehow we still seem to know each other deeply. We have truly been with each other in the silence. Amidst our conversations and words oneness is often easily lost. Amidst the silence, oneness can grow. My experience has been that in the silence we remember that we are indeed one in Christ, connected beyond all that separates. We have sunk deeper than the external surface of things into our hearts, and there we discover it is the same with us all.

Of course the world won't function in the silence. That would be naive to think so. But we can learn from the silence with a wish to fulfill Jesus' request for our oneness. We can bring more of the silence and the fruit of our silence into the world and all our interactions and obligations there. It is very difficult to disagree with someone in the silence. And it is also easier to simply be with someone different from us in the silence, beyond the demands of talking, especially if we don't speak the same language – figuratively or literally.

The gift of a meditative prayer practice such as Centering Prayer or the Jesus Prayer is that it draws us into the oneness of God's love connecting us with others in the solitude of our hearts where we can discover our sameness, our common humanity. All this has been said before. Poetic words for oneness are common. What is not common are communities of devotion and practice that embody the oneness through the silence.

May Jesus' prayer come to be more and more fulfilled in this season of Lent, binding the world together in an age when we scarce can risk being torn apart. With 7 billion of us here on this planet, grasping for the same resources of food, clean water, health and living wages, surely the old boundaries that have separated us mean less and less when my breakfast cantaloupe came from Mexico and my t-shirt from Cambodia. We aren't separate any more. We are a whole earth, and with it comes many blessings, but also many risks. We are vulnerable to one another. What we do affects you. What you do affects us.

I close with the silence of space. A deepening relational understanding of humankind and our destiny bound together is one of the great gifts of this image, seen for the first time in our era. It is an image that changes everything. The image of the pearled white and blue earth suspended against the black velvet of deep space. We can no longer deny the central truth that no matter what the maps and borders and cultures say, we truly are One.

A Living Lent [Day 36] *Thursday*

╬

What are You Looking For?

"Then Jesus, knowing all that was to happen to him, came forward and asked them, 'For whom are you looking?' They answered, 'Jesus of Nazareth.' Jesus replied, 'I am he.'" - John 18. 4-5

We are a week away from Maundy Thursday, the night we remember the events recorded in John chapter 18. After supper, Jesus leads his disciples into the Kidron valley, just below the Temple area in a steep valley where a grove of olive trees provides solitude for prayer. In John's Gospel, this is the location of the betrayal. A detachment of Roman soldiers and perhaps Temple police finds Jesus in the Garden, tipped off by Judas of course, and arrests our Lord.

Here is where we find Jesus on Maundy Thursday. Giving himself away. After his supper and service of foot washing, after his high priestly prayer and beautiful theological declarations (John 13-17), Jesus doesn't panic, he simply asks a question: "For whom are you looking for?" And then gives himself away.

Notice that Jesus doesn't seem to mind giving himself away. He freely admits "I am the one you are looking for." I am Jesus of Nazareth. Understanding that to the religious power-brokers he was *just* a trouble maker from Nazareth, he demonstrates that he sees himself from their perspective. It is as if he says, "I know that you need to arrest me. I know you think of me as a problem to be solved. I know you are afraid. So, here I am. If you are *just* looking for Jesus of Nazareth, Jesus replies, "I am he." If you are just looking for something to do this Easter Sunday morning, then, I'm your guy.

But to those with open hearts and open minds, hungering for more than just a cultural event (like John and Mary of Bethany who both listen deeply to the Lord in a contemplative disposition) it is as if Jesus is saying, Yet if you are looking for love itself I will show you the Way. It is not a popular way though and it won't be easy. That's basically what he was saying to the thief on the cross, who understood that there was more to Jesus than just "that pesky religious guy from Nazareth causing a commotion with his successful preaching and miracle-ministry." The thief understood that Jesus was the Way to Ultimate Love, which is another way of saying paradise.

If we are looking for power, control, wealth, fame and adoration from our religious experience or even ministries, we will most likely get what we are looking for, at least in some form; especially if your church is in Texas, California or Florida, or so it would seem by reading the Christian magazine Outreach's recent special on "the Fastest, biggest" churches in America.

While the System got what it wanted – an arrested, crucified Jesus – Ultimate Love (i.e. God) always surprises and reminds us that with God, we need to be careful what we are looking for. There are many things to seek for that look like the Kingdom of God (i.e. success, fruition, etc.) but that may have little to do with the principles of the Kingdom of God. Many of us confuse our kind of king with God's kind of king, which is apparently to be willing to give everything away, not accumulate and control and gain and rise up and succeed and enhance and be blessed and be wealthy and healthy and everything else we might ask the "Santa Claus God in the sky" for.

You see, there is something more to look for than *just* the historical Jesus of Nazareth. There is something more to look for than successful ministry in Jesus' name. There is something more to look for than cultural dominance; there is something deeper than the surface of things that most people totally miss out on. Unless you ask. Unless you seek. Unless you knock. There is more to Jesus. There is also the Jesus that is inviting you to be what he was – a participant in the divine nature and to enter into the kingdom of God right now *in you*.

You'll miss out on the depth if you live on the surface fascinated with the "historical" Jesus and all that Jesus can do for you and your church. It seems to me that some American churches have become Empires of Commerce selling Jesus and a Jesus lifestyle, making hundreds of millions off the enterprise. More if you include all the books and music and movies and paraphernalia and leadership summits and life coaching. On and on the business of American "Jesus church" goes. From my perspective, the danger seems to be that it is secretly built upon looking for *just* the surface level, *just* the "Jesus of Nazareth" level, and not the *ultimate source of love* level, the Son of God level, the "I in you, and you in me" level, the "die to self and be raised in Christ" level.

I'm writing these words partly as a reminder to myself. It is good for my heart to ponder the question, "What am I looking for?" A life-boosting religion or philosophy for a successful life? Or, am I looking to become

Life itself? To become Love itself? To become a participant of the divine nature (2 Peter 1.4)?

It is inevitable that our popular media based culture will flock to the cool, hip and trendy messengers of success and spiritual tips for living and having our best life now. Especially if there is a concert like worship experience with mood lights and flat screen TV's flashing iMac generated graphics and videos and satellites connecting multi-site church "franchise" venues (nothing against iMacs).

Meanwhile ignoring and perhaps even mocking the ancient practices of silence and solitude and simplicity that help heal our False self and its addiction to power, success and always feeling great; ignoring to our detriment, the deepest experience of God's presence in the interior, contemplative dimension.

Perhaps I'm misguided in my perceptions; I certainly am not the last word on anything. Yet perhaps it is worthwhile to ponder and remember for a moment on the cusp of Holy Week that our Lord and Teacher willingly gave himself away – the opposite of accumulating power, wealth, success, and large attendance – topics that seem to dominate our attention, in my view, disproportionately and border on the very sin of Judas – betrayal for our own silvery gain.

A Living Lent [Day 37] *Friday*

╬

Questions

"Aren't you one of this man's disciples too?" - John 18.17

After Jesus' arrest, John chapter 18 reveals that his disciples, particularly Peter and John (anonymous in the text), follow Jesus to the High Priest's courtyard. Inside the house Jesus is interrogated. Outside by the fire, Peter, lead disciple is also put to the test. Peter is spotted, recognized and asked, "Hey, aren't you one of Jesus' disciples too?" He quickly answered, "No!" This was his first denial. The question is repeated, this time a relative of the person Peter struck with the sword in the Garden. Again, Peter replies "No!"

Meanwhile, inside Jesus is interrogated about his teachings (v.19), and about how he answers questions (v.22). He is asked several questions by Pilate: "Are you king of the Jews?" (v.33). "So you are a king!" (v.37), and famously, "What is the truth?" (v.38). The result of Pilate's private interrogation is legal innocence. Pilate finds no basis for the charges against Jesus' arrest.

And here is my question: Notice how questions are the problem here. Where do the questions come from but the disjointed, unharmonious human mind disconnected from the heart. Can we see how our own questions create a buffer between our personal experiences with the living Christ? Can we see how when the mind is solely in charge, with all its questions, it tries to remain in control and keep the situation fully understood? Can we see how we are only willing to believe so much? And can we see how such cold questions reveal a lack of warmth and openness to God, and in contrast, the presence of fear, judgment and even worse negative emotions such as hatred? The questions we ask reveal much about who we are and what is important to us.

Meanwhile, the heart knows beyond knowing and asks no questions, preferring to live by faith and love. And for all of us who are taking this literally, please don't. The mind is more than the brain. And the heart is more than the physical organ that pumps blood. Mind and heart are also language symbols representing the mysterious thinking and feeling dispositions of a human being.

People like John and Mary of Bethany demonstrate the harmonization of head and heart. People like Pilate reveal the friction that many of us feel between head and heart. While our heart says one thing, our mind tells us another. What will we believe?

Dreams are often the language of the "heart." Which is why Pilate's wife is such a messenger of deeper truth from the heart than Pilate's keen legal mind. Pilate can't reconcile his head and heart and goes with what is most pragmatic. He trades Jesus for a criminal and the story is set up for the Good Friday events.

Peter too shows that he has much inner development yet remaining on his spiritual journey. Overcome by fear, his rational mind takes over and he forgets the passion of his heart. He goes rational and denies one of his deepest truths – that he knows Jesus. Indeed, loves Jesus. How can such a denial be explained apart from the fact that we live in tension and juxtaposition between our head and heart, with our head often winning in moments of fear.

Jesus is *not* calling us to be anti-intellectual or non-rational. That is not what I am interested in either. What I am seeking is the awareness of our multiplicity and duplicity because we are often not in balance. We are out of balance, completely in our heads, where fear and greed and survival and power speak a compelling language. Perhaps I might even say Western Civilization is stuck in the head.

In the heart, as we discover in meditative prayer, we remember who we are and that nothing can separate us from the love of God in Christ, including our own thoughts, questions, feelings, moods and any external situation that is occurring in our lives.

The heart knows implicitly that we are his disciples. The mind can't comprehend or explain it completely. This is why we pray "Thy kingdom come on earth as it is in heaven." In one sense, earth is our mind, heaven is our heart. Looking at it this way, we are praying for the harmonization and fusion of our head and heart. This fusion is represented by various symbols integrating the higher and lower. Such as:

and:

In both cases, the fusion of intelligence and intuition is represented by two dimensions coming into union.

In the instance of the cross the horizontal beam fuses with the vertical. In the case of the Star of David, the upper triangle fuses with the lower triangle. Symbols. Powerfully conveying many meanings, like dreams, but ultimately this is the essence of faith: the fusion of intelligence and intuition into pure wisdom and love.

A Living Lent [Day 38] *Saturday*

A Different Kingdom

"My Kingdom is not from this world." - John 18.36

Jesus Christ is not helping himself with a statement like this. In a trial like setting with his life on the line defending oneself by saying (in our modern understanding) that you're from another planet or from a different dimension of space is probably not the best approach. But the Christ seems to not only be from a different place than earth, but also to be on a different mission. His statement is meant to shock the ruling elite with a reminder of scale – yes, scale. The scale of Being. His statement was a shock to remind them that there is scale in the creation and that this planet – much less any nation – is not the center of the universe. In fact, it is just one place among billions and billions of other places in the universe.

It is as if Jesus is saying: "you think you are very powerful. You think what concerns you is of utmost importance: keeping control, gaining power, growing wealth. I'm not from here and where I am from these are not of concern. These are earth concerns. These are human pursuits. There is so much more to the universe and to existence then your petty power squabbles and pursuits for control on this earth and its kingdoms. I'm here to remind you that there is something more to live for than preserving your own power. I'm here to show you the Kingdom of God."

When we don't understand the reality of scale in the creation we tend to collapse everything to our experience here on planet earth. Scale of Being, like the musical scale, teaches us that there is a lower and a higher, and that they are interrelated and connected, and that we are invited to grow and develop our Being.

✠ Holy Week

"I suppose no soul of any sensitiveness can live through Holy Week without an awed and grateful sense of being incorporated in a mystery of self-giving love which yet remains far beyond our span."

-   Evelyn Underhill, *"Light of Christ"*

A Living Lent [Day 39]
Palm Sunday

╬

Beginning Holy Week

On this Palm Sunday we remember Jesus' joyful reception into the city he loved, the city of peace, Jerusalem. Yet what does this mean for our spiritual lives?

The contemplative dimension invites us to see the city of Jerusalem as a symbol for the center of our world – that is, our heart. The scriptures speak of Jerusalem as a city of compact unity (Psalm 122.3). Can you see the connection between the human heart? Jerusalem represents our emotional center, where we may receive or reject the Christ. Today, we celebrate liturgically the moment of history when Jesus actually did enter the literal Jerusalem. We also celebrate the ongoing spiritual opportunity to receive Christ into the center of our life, the spiritual Jerusalem, the city of potential peace dwelling in each of us.

The players involved in the unfolding drama of Jesus' Passover week are well-known. Who will we listen to? Which dimension will guide our inner life – the warm welcome of love or the rejection by fear?

I have recalled many of such ways of being (i.e. players of the drama) in the previous daily reflections throughout the season of Lent. Now, we take the final turn into the depths of this spiritual season of waiting and watching. Holy week begins today. Holy week is always beginning. Always welcoming us to receive, listen, suffer,

[130]

die and be raised again to life. Over and over again, this pattern is played out spiritually in our lives. Please know I'm not talking literally. I'm talking about the spiritual journey of dying to self and being raised deeper into Christ.

May each day of this holy week reveal more of who God is inviting us to become in Christ. May this holy week be more than just one more journey through the liturgical cycle.

May it be a true participation in the life of Christ, who for us and our salvation absorbed the fullness of the human condition in all its violent depths so to lift human nature all the way to the heart of Abba, becoming a fount of healing for all who simply say Yes.

A Living Lent [Day 40] *Monday*

The End of Violence

"They kept coming up to him...and striking him on the face." - John 19.3

Our Lenten journey arrives in holy week. It is a week of preparations – for Passover and now for the remembrance of Jesus' Passion.

Our fasting and increased spiritual practices in lent have all meant to prepare us for the deepest participation in the events of this week. If you have not prepared this lent, that is ok. The present moment is a perfect time to begin.

We turn to John chapter 19 today, nearing the climax of Jesus Passion which culminates with the releasing of his spirit recorded by the Gospel with these beautiful phrases, "it is finished" (John 19.30) and "into your hands I commend my spirit" (Luke 23.46).

My attention is drawn to this simple phrase, *"and striking him on the face"* (John 19.3). In my previous readings of the Gospel, I seem to have missed that detail. It conveys the very personal emotion of anger and disdain toward Jesus.

If you watch strangers fight, they often concentrate on attacking the other's body. But family members or lovers or friends, will often focus on attacking the other's face, throat or eyes. There is something so intimate about the face – even in our fighting and violence.

The face is the place where we meet the world and the world meets us most personally. It is through the countenance of Jesus that people were both deeply drawn to him and deeply repulsed by him. Perhaps the world can't handle such beauty as reflected in the face of Jesus, as of the Father's only son. And so it was struck. During this holy week, I'm going to intentionally write briefer reflections to pare our attention more keenly on the story and not my commentary.

So, I conclude with this reflection and question: the face of love and innocence is profoundly attractive and mysteriously also profoundly infuriating to others. Just think of all the victims of injustice who have surrendered to their perpetrators. It is as if their willingness made them more beautiful and provoked a deeper rage. As if anger was trying somehow to get under their gaze of peace and disturb. Of course, pure love cannot be disturbed by even the most violent of rages. I'm thinking not only of Jesus, but also of victims of hate crimes like during the Selma marches or the dragging of Matthew Shephard or of countless husbands raging against their wives' faces and then in the next moment trying to manipulate their behavior with the contorted words, "but I love you" as portrayed recently so well in the movie Safe Harbor.

The thing is (and this is one of the hardest things on the spiritual journey) to see in yourself this same kind of rage and anger and hatred. You may not act on it, as some have or do, but it is very important to recognize the parts of our self that also wish to strike the innocent in the

[133]

face in our moments of very negative emotions, such as hatred, anger and disdain. Can you see this in yourself? It is humbling to do so, but also very freeing because you can begin to also experience that the love of Jesus is reaching out not just to his abusers, but to the whole human condition in me, in you, in all of us. And in his absorbing of the worst of the human condition in its expressions of violence Jesus was healing it, so to give what he obtained back to us in a transfusion of grace enabling us to truly be "new creations" (2 Corinthians 5.17-21), no longer held captive by the power of anger, rage and violence. No longer heirs to the kingdom of violence, but now also heirs to the kingdom of peace, the true Jerusalem of our transformed hearts.

A Living Lent [Day 41] *Tuesday*

╬

What If Pilate Didn't Fear?

"When Pilate heard this he was more afraid than ever." - John 19.8

Fear invites reactive thinking. Fear is the opposite of love. Fear is a primitive emotion rooted in our limbic brain, useful for our survival and also very destructive in the delicate movements of human development. A fear based rage by a parent or teacher toward a young child may mark that child's development for a lifetime – or until good therapy can help release the clutched cells of the body constricted so long ago in the face of perceived danger.

Pilate's judicious mind was gripped in fear. Whatever openness may have been possible to Jesus up until that moment, now evaporated for good. Fear smothers openness. Fear closes options. Fear shuts us down deep into primitive fight and flight, either/or thinking. There is no subtlety or grace in the presence of fear. Only the severity of black or white extremist thinking. Right or wrong. This or that. Mercy has no room to stretch its wings and soar under the heavy gravity of fear. It is like an ocean of pressure hanging over our heads, and we swoon under its darkness, losing all sense of rationality.

Poor Pilate was in a bind. Caught by the Jewish legal loop-hole of a prisoner swap, and the clear innocence of love and wisdom in the person of Jesus. Perhaps another week he would not have felt so much pressure. Perhaps the crowds and the thousands of pilgrims intensified his sense of fear. What if the crowds get out of control? It is my job on the line and I'm accountable to Rome. What if I lose control of the Temple or if the Jewish leadership turns on me? In the presence of such stark options, clearly the way of least resistance was to solve the legal and social problem by getting rid of this intriguing but underwhelming peasant Rabbi from up North. It would only cost him a little water and soap, washing his hands of the dilemma forever – or so he thought.

Fear. It drives the world away from God and into solutions of our own making. The trouble is fear based solutions often take an inner toll upon our psyche that can't be calculated beforehand. One might think Peace is the opposite of Fear. But we are reminded by scripture that *"perfect love casts out fear"* (1 John 4.18). The cure for fear is love. Not sappy love. But the kind of love in which one knows and feels that nothing can separate you from God. That is the unmovable kind of love that fosters faith in the presence of fear and begins to shift our brain functioning upward from our reptilian limbic reactivity into the higher functioning of the neocortex, the most developed dimension of our triune brain.

By the way, I'm not talking about the technical term *"the fear of the Lord is the beginning of wisdom"* (Proverbs 9.10). That is better translated as *the right thinking or reverence of God is the beginning of wisdom*. Even better: correct thinking about oneself and God begins in the understanding that God is from a higher/deeper dimension than us, and therefore we live in awe and humility because we clearly see our place in the vast order of reality. That is a different kind of "fear" than what Pilate was experiencing.

If fact, the source of Pilate's fear was exactly the loss of the fear of the Lord. That is to say, Pilate began to take himself too seriously, overly identifying with his role, he forgot there was a higher dimension to appeal too – higher than his political office, higher than the religious power of the Temple, law and its leadership – the very source of Being, Life, Love and Wisdom, and this Source was, ironically, hiding in plain sight right before him in the form of a common man with an uncommon quality of fearlessness rooted in his faith and sense of oneness with his Abba.

What if Pilate didn't fear? It is a lesson for humankind in fear based outcomes, and an invitation to follow a different path, the path of love.

A Living Lent [Day 42] *Wednesday*

⟊⟊

Writing about the Crucifixion, Is like an Ant Trying to Read Shakespeare

"So they took Jesus and carrying the cross by himself, he went out to what is called The Place of the Skull, which in Hebrew is called Golgotha." - John 19.17

Writing about the crucifixion I feel like an ant trying to read Shakespeare. It is not that the story is hard to understand. It is actually starkly straightforward. Trumped up, fear-based charges lead to a short shrift trial that ends with a death sentence, in the traditional Roman execution style of crucifixion.

Jesus is not the only criminal executed that day (Luke 23.39-43). On each side of Jesus' cross, is another condemned man. To his left, perhaps, a person who sees in Jesus, pure innocence. To his right, the person who can't see anything more to Jesus other than another disappointment. He sees the cruelty of life, and so mocks Jesus' claims. The man probably died bitter and angry. There, in the middle, is Jesus, in between the human polarity of judgment and mercy.

The triad of the three crosses represents in symbolic form the movement of love entering into life. In response to such love, two options emerge. The first is resistance. The second is surrender, or what I call mercy.

Mercy is such a sweet friend. She moves with a calm delicacy stronger than death. She wakes the hopeless and teaches the blind to see. She keeps me up at night and puts my body to sleep. She sings ancient songs; her words become my tears of healing. She walks in the moonlight shades telling of a distant sun. And her name is bright in that darkness, silent behind the songs of every generation sung to our dirge of birth and futility, and the earth's risings toward the heart of Everlasting Desire.

I listen to Bach a lot in Holy Week. Particularly "Come Sweet Death." It is not morose, but it is honest. The problem with life on this planet isn't death, or even the crucifixion. The problem is that we think death won't happen to us. We think we aren't going to die, and for the most part, we live as if we won't. Until we realize we will. Then, like that right criminal we often get angry at God. While we lived our life as if God didn't exist, we suddenly grow angry at God. Ignore God in the day and rail against God at night. It is a funny all too common rhythm of the human heart.

The middle cross of the triad crucifixion event of Jesus the Christ on the Skull-hill a sling-shot's throw from the Temple is the in-breaking of love between the extremes of mercy and judgment. How that middle cross is love is a mystery only Eternal Desire can explain. It is a hinge to hang the swinging door between life and death. To one side, paradise. To the other, nothingness.

The Skull. Cracked open revealing two hemispheres of thought and being. We, the split brain beings. We, the two brained, double minded beasts of Ruah rising upward toward the light like moths in a jungle on a full moon night. Will we get the message? Can we see the absurding of our thinking as we play the drama of scape-goating the innocent hung up on the stage for all poor players to see the sound and fury of our ant tribes marching like little gods to tombs of self-made kingdoms only to find them empty, but full of distraction? It is indeed a tale told by an idiot, slurking in the dust waiting for that middle-beamed heel of love to crack its reptilian skull open to the light.

A Living Lent [Day 43]
Maundy Thursday

╬

Finished, We Begin

"It is finished." - John 19.30

Maundy Thursday evening begins the three-day journey called the *Easter Triduum.* That is Latin for "three days," including our remembrance of Jesus' Last Supper, the crucifixion on Good Friday, and Resurrection on the third day. Remember that in the biblical era the day ended and began at sunset. So the Last Supper on Thursday night is the first day that ends with his burial on Friday. The second day is Holy Saturday. And the third day is Resurrection Sunday.

Today, we complete John chapter 19 by focusing on Jesus' cry from the cross, *"it is finished!"* An important question to ask is this: *what* is finished? On the surface, it looks like Jesus' life is finished. This is the cry of a man giving up his spirit consciously. In other words, it is as if Jesus is saying, my journey is complete. But is there more to it than that?

Looking deeper, we may also begin to discern that what is finished is not *just* Jesus' physical life, but also the divine experiment and plan of going all the way into the depths of the human condition, including its God-forsakeness and violence. Jesus is saying, the experiment is done. I've reached the end point of the human line. I've carried the Father's Divine love all the way down into the depths of the human condition. And like a seed planted in the darkness, now we await to see what will be born. We are still waiting for its full flourishing which is why we continue to pray, "Thy kingdom come."

An ancient theologian put it this way: that which was not assumed (i.e. experienced) was not healed. In other words, in order for the whole human condition to be healed, the whole human condition needed to be assumed and experienced. So, what Jesus is saying is that the mission of assuming all of the human condition is complete. Divine love has assumed and absorbed the whole human spectrum from birth to death, including the utmost expression of sin: the violent rejection of love in the name of righteousness.

The incarnational journey of Jesus's divine-human body is now ending. It is complete. While several more journeys await Jesus, those journeys involve a different dimension of time and space, and probably also a different form of his own physical being: His descent into hell. His return to the Father. His resurrection from the dead. His ascension from this planet. And his future return to this planet.

The benefit of Jesus' complete journey into the fullness and depths of the human condition is that there is now nothing limiting us (i.e. separating us) from God's love. When we enter into relationship with Christ, that is, when we are united to the divine nature by faith, we begin to receive the healing and wholeness he also experienced on our behalf. We begin to receive the transfusion of the healed human nature he obtained through his absorbing it.

Jesus took on human nature to heal it. And like a beautiful process of transfusion through word and sacrament, this transfusion becomes personal and available to us. We move from death to life, old to new; from being separated from God to being united in God through Christ by the Spirit. Because it is finished, we can begin again.

A Living Lent [Day 44]
Good Friday

A Friday Terror become Good

Today is Good Friday. Words will be in abundance in sermons and homilies trying to explain how such a terrible experience of suffering and death as the cross can be called good.

Perhaps this, more than any other day in the liturgical life of the church, is a day for silence. And perhaps that was the intuition of the earth and maybe even the cosmos when it wore silence in the dress of darkness during the dying hours of Jesus.

I don't think that is a narrative dramatic flourish. I think that is an insight into the cracking open of the system of violence by the presence and pressure of love.

Jesus' body was the location of this atomic collision between light and darkness at a cellular level – divine love and justice colliding with sin and violence absorbed by the body of Jesus. He's like a lightning rod hung between heaven and earth absorbing the virus of human violence like a sponge, releasing it back to God and us with prayers, tears and forgiveness.

As in the opening scene of creation the Spirit hovered over the chaos, so too in the darkness of Golgotha the Spirit hovers over this hypostatic super-collider of light and darkness in the body of Jesus. This is an event that can't be undone. It is a restart for the cosmos. It is the

Ruah downdraft of Divine love hitting the rock bottom of human nature, so to lift it up into the Omega wholeness of Christ. The rescue mission is complete. The severe downdraft of God in Christ is cracking the system open to save us from ourselves.

Thankfully, the Spirit doesn't stop with the hovering over the collision between light and darkness, life and death, violence and innocence. Spirit also continues the movement of love by raising human destiny to completion with resurrection, releasing the unconquerable light and life of Christ into the universe.

The Word is still speaking from the tomb of silence. Will we listen? That is one way such a Friday terror became good.

A Living Lent [Day 45]
Holy Saturday

From Womb to Tomb, Mary

"Early on the first day of the week, while it was still dark, Mary Magdalene came to the tomb and saw that the stone had been removed from the tomb." - John 20.1

On Holy Saturday the church awaits in silence for the celebration of resurrection on Easter Sunday. Sanctuaries all around the world are empty today, silent and at rest. It is a symbol of reverence to Jesus who was also at rest in the dark tomb, awaiting the incomprehensible completion of his spiritual journey. We await, as if on vigil for the paschal light of the world to return.

It is interesting to note the similarities between Jesus' birth from the womb of Mary celebrated at Christmas, and Jesus' "second birth" from the tomb of death first announced and experienced by Mary Magdalene celebrated at Easter. From womb to tomb, Christmas to Easter, Jesus was nurtured by Marys. Perhaps there really is something about Mary.

Mary Magdalene represents the impulse of love and devotion in all of us. She, like Jesus' mother, understood Jesus. She loved him. And Jesus loved her.

In one sense, the main character in this scene isn't Jesus or Mary – it is the empty tomb. Since at first there is no interaction with Jesus or an angel, just the empty tomb and Mary. There are fine legal analyses of the veracity of the resurrection accounts. By all appearances and logic, there is sound reason to believe the best explanation for the behavior of the disciples prior to and after Jesus' resurrection is that it really did happen. Of course there are alternative accounts and explanations. People have been dismissing the resurrection from the beginning. For me, I don't just believe in the resurrection. I know it. I experience it. It means everything to me.

What I mean has to do with the interior experience of discovering my heart as the cave-tomb of resurrection. This involves the early hours of the day. It often requires the darkness, literally and metaphorically. It involves the silence. Waiting. Resting with the name of Jesus in the inner chamber of my heart. And then experiencing the presence of the living Jesus Christ. This is also the intent of the real presence of Christ in Communion/Eucharist. Christ's presence involves our attention and consent.

It also involves a desire: I am interested in becoming more like Mary Magdalene. Eager to be nearer to Christ. She had no idea Jesus wasn't going to be in the tomb. She just wanted to be near him. Perhaps even speak to Jesus as we so often do when we visit the graveside of our beloved ones who have passed away and rest in the earth.

Perhaps in the darkness and quiet of that early morning, she hoped to sit beside the tombstone, and just be near Jesus. Perhaps she also remembered his words and hoped that he really would rise. Perhaps she intuited that his life was not really over, and that there was more to come. Perhaps she felt his living presence and was awoken from sleep, compelled to go to the tomb and see what she knew to be true already in her heart, but not yet comprehending with her mind.

Mary Magdalene perceived beyond the surface of things into the inner movements of mystery, and followed her heart to the tomb to wait and watch. As it turns out, she was right. She is an example of the contemplative disposition, and we can all learn from her way of life. Listening. Loving. Rising early. Praying the name of Jesus in our hearts. Waiting in the darkness and silence for the Beloved to return and speak.

A Living Lent [Day 46]
Easter Sunday

The Deeper Spell of Resurrection

We conclude our 46 day Lenten journey today, Easter Sunday. I'm writing after a full day of worship services – 6:00 am sunrise, 9:00 am traditional and 11:00 am contemporary.

It is nearing the end of the day. I've been reflecting on the resurrection since dawn. The day began with low hanging fog, melting snow on the fields and a hidden sun. During the second hymn of the 9:00 am service, the sun broke through the clouds and lit the sanctuary in golden light. It was a beautiful moment and I will always cherish this, my first Easter at Westminster. A cold front blew through around noon and the wind has been fierce from the north, bringing a clear blue sky. The sunset will be beautiful tonight.

During the sunrise service, I preached on the miracle of the resurrection. Since resurrection is not something we experience on this planet, we have a hard time believing that it actually happened. Far too many of our loved ones have died and been buried with the shadow of that ancient resurrection seemingly doing nothing for them. We often wonder why resurrection doesn't happen more often. Why is it just reserved for Jesus and not grandpa? It is not a matter of the quality of the miracle. It is a matter of quantity of time. It simply requires more

[149]

time for humankind to be ready to receive the Omega Point of Jesus' ancient resurrection come to meet us in the final resurrection at the end of time. Until then, we ponder the miraculous nature of Jesus' resurrection.

Miracles are disruptions in the common and ordinary laws of planet earth. They are laws from a higher dimension, over-ruling our lower laws, in a similar way a 5 star General over-rules the will and functioning of a Private first class soldier. Remembering that we are in an ordered, hierarchical universe is an important first step in being open to the possibility of miracles and especially the resurrection. When our life and our planet are not at the center, and we are "below" the "beyond." From that perspective of submission, it becomes possible to begin to see that what we think of as normal and lawful on this planet are not the last words or full embodiment of possibilities in the totality of possible universes. Remember, Jesus said we must be born again from above – that is to say, from a higher dimension, a fuller level of Being.

Resurrection is simply the suspension of the normal laws of this world – especially the law of cause and effect and the law of suffering, sickness and death. Such laws are suspended in the presence of deeper laws from higher dimensions of the universe(s) or beyond, such as the law of infinite supply, health and abundant life. This is all possible on the God level.

I close with a quote from author C.S. Lewis. He said, some spells are only broken by a deeper spell. The spell of death is broken by the deeper spell of resurrection. And once it occurred, it is now released in this realm changing everything. And time is a factor.

Jesus' resurrection was similar to D-day. It did not defeat death for all instantaneously. It announced the sure and certain V-day forthcoming. Jesus' resurrection is the "first fruits" of a fuller summer blooming. Jesus is the first-born among a large family. We await V-day when the spell of resurrection reaches every cell of the universe and speaks it back into the *pleroma* (i.e. abundant fullness) of Christ, for which Jesus came to show us the Way into.

Every blessing on your journey deeper into the ever expanding cosmos of God's love. It is, I think and feel, what a lifetime is for.

✚ *Postscript*

Life in Christ
Every Day

Continuing the Journey

While Lent may end, the spiritual journey continues. I'm writing this postscript the morning after a weekend seminar with contemplative author Bernadette Roberts. The seminar was really an extended conversation on the Mystery of Christ, and the joyous invitation of humankind to become Christ.

If you are interested in continuing the Christian spiritual journey beyond the daily devotions of Lent, and wish to go deeper into the life and love of the Trinity, I think a meaningful best next step might be to get a copy of Bernadette's new book *The Real Christ*. Though profoundly deep and challenging, I believe it is the single most important book to read for contemplatives to understand where Christianity lost the beauty of WHAT Christ is and HOW we can participate in the Christ Life.

Perhaps I'm not the only one who is happy to experience the magnificent joy of realizing the end of all our journeys is simply being in God in Christ?

☩ *Contemplative Prayers for Ash Wednesday & Holy Week*

Ash Wednesday

God of Transformation:

You set our hearts on fire with the personal touch of your Spirit enfolding truth into our minds as an impression of wisdom.

You enliven us with your love that we know beyond knowing. Your unstoppable impulse to share your life with us is available to us at this moment.

Amen.

Palm Sunday

And now, O God of perfect timing, enter into each of our hearts and find the city-center in us ready to receive and surrender to your love in its embodied form and in its eternal formlessness.

We have been preparing for the entrance of your Word through this Lenten journey and now we feel your timeless approach nearing. What are you calling us to do? What more can we surrender of our self? How can we live with this exquisite wound of love that suffering teaches?

This city-center is the ongoing temple of our heart, mind, and soul, today arranged and set apart to celebrate your arrival.

Your way shows us that soon your arrival will require surrender, and in this surrender there will be great suffering.

Yet, so too your truth shows us that in this suffering there will be something gained on behalf of others, and through this gain of love a power untold will pierce through the field of appearances and birth a new life through all that is dead and dying in us.

And so it is that your life is felt more fully in our welcoming all things, but especially the body and blood of the Eucharist as the ongoing teacher and embrace of your joyful presence.

Amen.

Maundy Thursday

Lord God of All Creation:

Every night reminds us of the darkness that we can't escape, yet tonight the darkness is particularly deep.

Infused with betrayal, laced with denial, sealed with the cup, marked with Gethsemane blood, you, Lord Jesus Christ, embraced surrender while rejecting the way of the sword. You entered into the valley of the shadow of death, meeting betrayal, denial, rejection, conviction, abandonment in order to join human nature in the depths of its dysfunction and rejection of love.

If evil is the denial of the reality of God, then sin is a way of life based on the unreality of God, who is love. Tonight, we prepare to see the depths of unreality: unbelief, hatred, and violence.

Lord Jesus, the drama is enacted in your life to show us what is in our life, and in its exposing to the light of your surrendering yet pursuing love, we hear the clank of keys coming down the dark prison hallway of the night that lets the prisoners know they can be free. It sounds like this: "Father, forgive them for they know not what they do."

Amen.

Good Friday

My God, My God of All My Why's:

It is now finished. This is the hour. The moment when selfhood became lost into your hands, and your hands became remembered in a human body. One with you in Jesus, humanity can never be separated again.

I need not wonder how it is done, only request the grace to surrender to let it be done unto me: dead to self, alive to you.

Amen.

Holy Saturday

Lord Jesus, Living Christ:

On your inward journey into the depths of being and beyond, reveal in each of us the places where there are still captives that need to hear your story and be set free. Descend all the way down into the thinking and doing that is resistant to your love. We need your help to be raised back to life not just tomorrow but right now, finally set free from our self-bound ways of fear and falseness. From that moment of integration with your love, we will truly live. You are indeed our hope of true glory, then, now, and always.

Amen.

Easter Sunday

O God of the Light, Bearer of the Heavens:

Your life, light, and love have once and for all permeated through the veil of human flesh into the fullness of the cosmos through the personal location of resurrection in the historical human Jesus of Nazareth. We wish to participate in that ongoing flourishing of human nature in union with the resurrection of Christ, pouring out into the realm of human relationships interconnected with you by the Spirit through the Eucharist and the mystery of oneness.

In our world of death, suffering, and sorrow, you have sounded a new octave of life, reverberating through the cosmos in each dimension and direction. Give to each of us the full capacity to consent to this signal sound permeating with the harmonics of love, seen and unseen. We wish to not only hear it but be the very vessel in which the sound is turned into form.

When this truthful sound lands in each of us, stabilize us with the wisdom of Scripture and the strength of community so that we are not undone by the glory of the event. Show us the way in our study and encounter with the living Christ through our silence in prayer and exclamation in praise. In, through and with Christ, for the hope of the creation and all whose hearts are warmed by the touch of love; who know beyond knowing that nothing can separate us from the love of God in the risen and ever living Christ.

Amen.

‡ *Contemplative Resources*

Books

Open Mind, Open Heart, by Thomas Keating

The Better Part, by Thomas Keating

A Beautiful Prayer by Peter Traben Haas

Centering Prayers by Peter Traben Haas

The God Who Is Here by Peter Traben Haas

Web

ContemplativeOutreach.org

ContemplativeChristians.com